JOURNAL FOR THE STUDY OF THE NEW TESTAMENT
SUPPLEMENT SERIES
30

Executive Editor, Supplement Series
David Hill

Publishing Editor
David E Orton

JSOT Press
Sheffield

Early Christian Rhetoric and 2 Thessalonians

Frank Witt Hughes

Journal for the Study of the New Testament
Supplement Series 30

For

Mary Witt Hughes, M.D., F.A.C.S.

Published by JSOT Press
JSOT Press is an imprint of
Sheffield Academic Press Ltd
The University of Sheffield
343 Fulwood Road
Sheffield S10 3BP
England

Printed in Great Britain
by Billing & Sons Ltd
Worcester

British Library Cataloguing in Publication Data

Hughes, Frank W.
    Early Christian rhetoric and 2
    Thessalonians.
    1. Bible. N.T. Thessalonians - Critical
    studies
    I. Title   II. Series
    227'.8106

ISSN 0143-5108
ISBN 1-85075-137-4

CONTENTS

Foreword by George A. Kennedy   7

Preface   9
Abbreviations   11

Chapter 1
2 THESSALONIANS AND HISTORICAL CRITICISM   13

Chapter 2
THE RHETORIC OF LETTERS   19

Chapter 3
A RHETORICAL INTERPRETATION
OF 2 THESSALONIANS   51

Chapter 4
2 THESSALONIANS AS A DEUTEROPAULINE LETTER   75

Chapter 5
CONCLUSIONS: THE LEGACY OF PAUL   97

Notes   105
Bibliography   131
Index of Biblical References   147
Index of Other Ancient and Mediaeval Literature   150
Index of Modern Authors   153

FOREWORD

When the late Henry Cadbury was teaching the New Testament at Harvard some thirty-five years ago, a student of classical Greek in his seminar proposed that an interpretive problem might be approached by emending the accent on one Greek word. Professor Cadbury, with a twinkle in his eye, conferred privately with the divinity students in the class and then announced, 'We have decided that the accents are not inspired!' The point of the story as I apply it here is that in understanding ancient texts as their original audiences received them we need to open our ears to the range of things they might have heard. When early Christians heard a letter of Saint Paul read to a congregation what they heard was a Greek letter, and to share their experience we need to understand their expectations of how a letter was composed: What were the conventions of letter-writing at the time? Those expectations and the audience's reactions to the text are a part of the phenomenon of rhetoric as diffused through the societies of the Greek-speaking world of the eastern Mediterranean, an integral part of the culture that permeated the language even to the level of those who were not formally literate.

It is a difficult challenge to enter into the cultural codes of distant times and places and a challenge that cannot fully be met. Much of our understanding of Hellenistic society has to be intuited from unexpressed assumptions in texts or physical remains hypothetically reconstructed by archaeologists. But in the case of the rhetorical code we do have a substantial body of theoretical writings that tells us about how texts, secular or sacred, were composed, transmitted and interpreted. Until fairly recently this source of insight was little used by biblical scholars. Saint Paul himself, for his own rhetorical purposes, had encouraged the view that rhetoric was something practiced by other people, and rhetoric was often dismissed by early twentieth-century scholars as a matter of the artificial adornment of style. In the last fifteen years, in their search for new methodologies

to explicate a small corpus of precious texts, biblical scholars have
rediscovered rhetoric and begun to make significant advances in
opening our ears to an ancient discourse.

Frank Witt Hughes has, it seems to me, made a valuable
contribution to the process of rediscovery in this new book. By taking
a broad understanding of rhetoric at the outset he has avoided one
flaw apparent in some rhetorical studies where scholars have seized
upon a single aspect of theory taken out of context and constructed
an interpretation that is inconsistent with the tenor of the work as a
whole. His study is unusually interesting in moving its focus of
attention into the dynamics of controversy found in the writings of
Saint Paul's followers in the generation after his death, a crucial
period in the development of Christianity where we have little other
information. I hope that others will find this new study as
informative and convincing as I have.

George A. Kennedy
Paddison Professor of Classics
University of North Carolina at Chapel Hill

PREFACE

It is a pleasure to acknowledge the contribution of many scholars who have read and commented on earlier versions of this work, especially Robert Jewett, Dennis E. Groh, Michael C. Leff, Thomas B. Farrell, O.C. Edwards, Jr, W. Richard Stegner, Wolfgang M.W. Roth, John J. Collins, Jonathan A. Goldstein, Edgar Krentz, David M. Hay, Karl P. Donfried, Wilhelm Wuellner, William Baird, J. Christian Wilson, David E. Knorr, and K. William Whitney, Jr. I thank all of them, and none of them should be held responsible either for the positions I hold or the mistakes which remain.

I also wish to thank several colleagues in religious studies who have made my life easier in various ways and have encouraged me to persevere in research and study, especially James Burnell Robinson, Martha J. Reineke and Paul B. Courtright. I am particularly grateful to Gerd Lüdemann, director of the Institute of Early Christian Studies in Göttingen, the Council for the International Exchange of Scholars in Washington, and the Fulbright-Kommission in Bonn for their cooperation in providing a Fulbright research grant for the academic year 1986-87.

My greatest debt continues to be to members of my family who have made it possible for me to pursue my vocation despite many seemingly insuperable obstacles. Chief among them is my mother Mary Witt Hughes, whose life exemplifies true liberation in the service of others. To her I dedicate this book.

F.W.H.
Göttingen
July 1987

ABBREVIATIONS

AB	Anchor Bible
AGJU	Arbeiten zur Geschichte des antiken Judentums und des Urchristentums
ATR	*Anglican Theological Review*
AusBR	*Australian Biblical Review*
BBB	Bonner biblische Beiträge
BCE	before the common era
BFCT	Beiträge zur Förderung christlicher Theologie
BHT	Beiträge zur historischen Theologie
Bib	*Biblica*
BJRL	*Bulletin of the John Rylands Library*
BZNW	Beihefte zur Zeitschrift für die neutestamentliche Wissenschaft
CBQ	*Catholic Biblical Quarterly*
CE	common era
CNT	Commentaire du Nouveau Testament
ConBNT	Coniectanea Biblica, New Testament
EBib	*Etudes bibliques*
EKKNT	Evangelisch-Katholischer Kommentar zum Neuen Testament
ETL	*Ephemerides Theologicae Lovanienses*
EvQ	*Evangelical Quarterly*
ExpTim	*Expository Times*
FRLANT	Forschungen zur Religion und Literatur des Alten und Neuen Testaments
HNT	Handbuch zum Neuen Testament
HTKNT	Herders theologischer Kommentar zum Neuen Testament
HTR	*Harvard Theological Review*
ICC	International Critical Commentary
Int	*Interpretation*

JBL	*Journal of Biblical Literature*
JRH	*Journal of Religious History*
JSNT	*Journal for the Study of the New Testament*
JSOTS	Journal for the Study of the Old Testament Supplement Series
JTS	*Journal of Theological Studies*
LCL	Loeb Classical Library
MeyerK	Kritisch-exegetischer Kommentar über das Neue Testament
NCB	New Century Bible
NKZ	*Neue kirchliche Zeitschrift*
NovT	*Novum Testamentum*
NovTSup	Supplements to Novum Testamentum
NTA	Neutestamentliche Abhandlungen
NTD	Das Neue Testament Deutsch
NTS	*New Testament Studies*
PWSup	Supplement to Pauly-Wissowa, *Real-Encyclopädie der classischen Altertumswissenschaft*
RB	*Revue biblique*
RelSRev	*Religious Studies Review*
RGG	*Religion in Geschichte und Gegenwart*
RSR	*Recherches de science religieuse*
RHPR	*Revue d'histoire et de philosophie religieuses*
RHR	*Revue de l'histoire des religions*
RSPT	*Revue des sciences philosophiques et théologiques*
RNT	Regensburger Neues Testament
SBLDS	Society of Biblical Literature Dissertation Series
SNT	Studien zum Neuen Testament
TBü	Theologische Bücherei
TSK	*Theologische Studien und Kritiken*
TU	Texte und Untersuchungen
TLZ	*Theologische Literaturzeitung*
TZ	*Theologische Zeitschrift*
VC	*Vigiliae Christianae*
WUNT	Wissenschaftliche Untersuchungen zum Neuen Testament
ZNW	*Zeitschrift für die neutestamentliche Wissenschaft*
ZTK	*Zeitschrift für Theologie und Kirche*
ZWT	*Zeitschrift für wissenschaftliche Theologie*

Chapter 1

INTRODUCTION:
2 THESSALONIANS AND HISTORICAL CRITICISM

Introduction

Contemporary students of the Bible are accustomed to a practical division of the Pauline corpus into two basic groups: the letters St Paul probably did write, and the letters he probably did not write. Excluding the Letter to the Hebrews, which is anonymous, and excluding the Pastoral Letters, which few scholars now identify as Pauline, we are left with ten letters which through their traditional titles and the words of their texts claim for themselves Pauline authorship. Contemporary historical criticism gives a positive verdict on the Pauline authorship of at least seven of the remaining epistles, i.e. Romans, 1 and 2 Corinthians, Galatians, Philippians, 1 Thessalonians, and Philemon. The authorship of the remaining three documents, Ephesians, Colossians, and 2 Thessalonians, often referred to as the Deuteropauline letters, is the subject of much debate and controversy.

The least generally studied of these three documents is 2 Thessalonians, it seems. Perhaps the relative neglect of 2 Thessalonians should be attributed to the content of these three letters. Ephesians and Colossians can readily be read by modern readers as expressions of what a mature, even 'mellow' Paul might have written, or, indeed, what we should like him to have written. Colossians and Ephesians seem to espouse a theology which is thoroughly congenial to many contemporary Christians. These documents speak about a God whose salvation is relatively accessible to those who call themselves Christians. The key to salvation, according to these letters, is the right knowledge of what God in Christ has done to redeem Christians from the power of evil. Indeed Colossians tells its readers that sin, like an official verdict of condemnation against sinners, has been nailed to the cross, and that its defeat has been accomplished

(Col. 2.14-15). Ephesians shares with many of its readers an overwhelming concern for the unity of the church, using the Pauline metaphor of the Body of Christ which should be a single body having many members, who should all work for the upbuilding of that body (Eph. 4.1-16). Ephesians proclaims as a present reality what we would like the church to become.

The imaginative universe of 2 Thessalonians seems considerably less inviting to me. It proclaims a future divine revenge upon the enemies of the Christian faith, who are called 'wicked and evil persons' who hinder apostolic work, 'for not all are trustworthy' (2 Thess. 3.2). The author of 2 Thessalonians maintains that the present church is at best a *corpus mixtum*, a body whose true composition will be made generally known at a fiery Last Judgment on the Day of the Lord (1.10; 2.2). The letter allows its readers to conclude that believers in the heretical theology it attacks are victims of a 'delusion' (2.11) whereby they believed not in truth but 'rejoiced in unrighteousness' (2.12). Theological orthodoxy is our author's most important concern, a passion which seems to overwhelm the desire for Christian tolerance and solidarity (3.14). Those who hold to the heretical theology will receive a divine punishment of eternal banishment from the presence of God and Christ, for they 'did not know God nor obey the Gospel of our Lord Jesus' (1.8-9). For his readers who do obey the Gospel, presumably by their being 'called through our Gospel' (2.14), as well as their holding fast the 'traditions which you were taught through our word (*logos*) or letter' (2.15), our author promises eternal consolation in the future, but not before tribulations and sufferings in the present (1.5-7).

It seems quite paradoxical that our author should in 2.15 refer to 'our epistle' as a source of true doctrine, while an 'epistle as from us' (2.2) is a source of the false doctrine our author so strenuously opposes and warns against. This warning is even more paradoxical in the light of the close relationship between 1 and 2 Thessalonians, even though the tone and theological outlook of each of these letters are so remarkably different, as many commentators have noted and as I shall argue. If an interpreter wishes to defend Pauline authorship for both Thessalonian letters, he or she must somehow explain why so many important words and phrases from 1 Thessalonians are found in 2 Thessalonians and in the same relative order. Given Pauline authorship, the best explanation of the literary closeness of the two letters is that Paul wrote them both within a short span of time, so that Paul's repeated phrases came from a copy of his letter or from memory.

The closer in time, however, that the two letters are placed, the more difficult it becomes to explain the strong differences in tone, outlook, and especially theology. If Paul wrote both letters within months or weeks of each other, how can one account for the marked changes in the expectation of the Parousia and the attitude of the author towards the Thessalonian congregation? The usual strategy of defenders of Pauline authorship of both letters has been to minimize the theological differences between the two letters. One can well ask whether this strategy really explains the letters we have or, rather, explains them away.

An Overview of Scholarship

Since the middle of the seventeenth century, scholarly attention to the Second Letter to the Thessalonians has been focused on the relationship of 1 and 2 Thessalonians. Numerous hypotheses have been made for and against the historical order of the two letters to the Thessalonians and for and against Pauline authorship. On the basis of the content of 2 Thessalonians, particularly its second and third chapters, Hugo Grotius found it impossible that Paul could have written 2 Thessalonians after writing 1 Thessalonians, particularly in view of the fact that the authenticating signature of 2 Thess. 3.17, which the letter claims to occur 'in every letter' of Paul, is not found in 1 Thessalonians. Since Grotius found it unlikely that Paul would write a letter without the authenticating signature and then, very soon after the writing of the first letter, and to the same church, write another with the authenticating signature, and yet claim that all true letters of Paul had a similar authentication, he was forced to reverse their order by arguing that the canonical 2 Thessalonians was in fact the first letter of Paul to the Thessalonians, followed by the canonical 1 Thessalonians.[1]

Grotius's reversal of the order of the letters was necessitated because of his belief in Pauline authorship of the two letters. Beginning with Johann Ernst Christian Schmidt in 1801,[2] several scholars produced articles which argued against Pauline authorship of 2 Thessalonians.[3] Ferdinand Christian Baur argued against Pauline authorship of both of the Thessalonian letters.[4] Baur noted the marked literary relationship between 1 and 2 Thessalonians, and as he found 1 Thessalonians lacking in Pauline theological content, he argued that 1 Thessalonians was literarily dependent on 2 Thessalonians.

The issue of literary dependence was taken up by several scholars, most notably William Wrede,[5] who argued persuasively that the author of 2 Thessalonians, whose theology represented one of several kinds of 'Paulinism',[6] used 1 Thessalonians as a literary source in order to authenticate his new, ostensibly Pauline, letter. Wrede argued that the words 'in every letter' in 2 Thess. 3.17 most likely presupposed the collection of Pauline letters,[7] and that the letter as a whole presupposed a time in which 'the Apostle' had for the first time denoted an authority figure whose stamp of approval carried clout in his churches, an 'ideal, intangible, and uncontrollable canon',[8] and so Wrede dated 2 Thessalonians, using the letter of Polycarp to the Philippians as a *terminus ad quem*, at about 110 CE.[9]

In response to Wrede, several scholars have attempted to salvage Pauline authorship of 2 Thessalonians by means of elaborate theories of different addressees for the two letters.[10] Several twentieth-century commentators have argued in favor of Pauline authorship of both letters, either defending Pauline authorship on principle or because of what they understand to be scanty indications of Deuteropauline authorship.[11]

New Testament scholarship remains divided on the issues of the authorship and purpose of 2 Thessalonians. The view that 2 Thessalonians is a Deuteropauline letter has been argued in a variety of ways in the monograph and commentary by Wolfgang Trilling;[12] and Willi Marxsen has argued in a New Testament introduction and a recent commentary that 2 Thessalonians is a response to a kind of early Gnosticism, represented by the view that 'the Day of the Lord has already come' (2 Thess. 2.2).[13] A strong criticism that can be made of Trilling's and Marxsen's views is that they provide little historical foundation for exegesis. The larger question that their commentaries raise is, if Paul did not write 2 Thessalonians, what kind of person did and why? If, as their influential studies indicate, it is not probable that Paul wrote 2 Thessalonians, is it possible to understand 2 Thessalonians within the larger framework of Pauline tradition?

The Plan of this Book

This study examines the problems of the authorship and purpose of
2 Thessalonians. In this book I argue that 2 Thessalonians is best
understood as a Deuteropauline or pseudopauline letter. Chapter 2
examines the ways in which traditional structures of Graeco-Roman
rhetoric influenced the writing of ancient letters. Chapter 3 gives an
interpretation of 2 Thessalonians according to these traditions. In
Chapter 4 I argue that the emergence of the rhetoric of 2
Thessalonians is best explained by a theological conflict among
branches of Pauline Christianity after Paul's death, and that 2
Thessalonians is a polemical response to other Paulinists who teach a
fulfilled eschatology, which our author attacks by telling his readers
that this heretical theology comes from a forged Pauline letter or letters
(2.2). I identify the theology that our author attacks as a theology
underlying Colossians and Ephesians. Chapter 5 concludes this
study by advancing the implications that Deuteropauline authorship
of 2 Thessalonians has for the history of Pauline Christianity,
namely the multifaceted and complex nature of the Pauline legacy.

Chapter 2

THE RHETORIC OF LETTERS

Epistolary Rhetoric and the Pauline Corpus

The 'quest of the rhetorical Paul' is not a new search. Even during
the lifetime of Paul, his adversaries recognized that the letters of Paul
had a powerful persuasive effect. In 2 Cor. 10.10, Paul preserved a
negative comment of his enemies about himself: 'For they say, "His
letters are weighty and strong, but his bodily presence is weak, and
his speech is despicable"'. Thus the enemies of Paul were contrasting
the power of Paul's letters with the apparent weakness of his oratory.
This evaluation by Paul's enemies, however, ran counter to the usual
evaluation of the rhetorical effectiveness of letters as compared with
the physical presence and polished delivery of an orator. The greatest
Greek orator, Demosthenes, wrote in a letter, 'It is a difficult thing, I
know, for advice conveyed by letter to hold its ground, because you
Athenians have a way of opposing many suggestions without waiting
to understand them'.[1] Isocrates, the famous Greek teacher of
rhetoric, wrote at length in two of his extant letters about why he
preferred not to write letters, relating this in one instance mainly to
the non-understanding by the audience of the letter,[2] and in another
instance mainly to the letter's not having the prestige of the speaker
and devices of oral delivery.[3] Thus, if this negative attitude toward
letters was the general attitude by rhetors, Paul's enemies' contention
that Paul's letters were 'weighty and strong', though his physical
presence and oral delivery were weak, indicates Paul's letters were
understood as powerful documents of rhetoric by Paul's enemies.[4]

Since the first century, other writers have commented on Paul's
use of rhetoric, among whom the most prominent was St Augustine
of Hippo, a well-educated teacher of rhetoric and later a Christian
bishop and theologian. In his work *De doctrina Christiana*, book 4 of
which is a Christian rhetorical handbook which uses rhetorical
works by Cicero such as *De inventione* and *Orator* to describe early

Christian rhetoric, Augustine analyzed biblical literature and its rhetorical styles. He found, for example, that Paul used the device called *klimax* in Greek and *gradatio* in Latin in Rom. 5.3-5, as well as another ornament 'which our [Latin] writers call *membra* and *caesa*, and the Greeks call *kola* and *kommata*'. 2 Corinthians was offered by Augustine as an example of *refutatio*: 'Writing to the Corinthians in the second epistle he refutes certain persons, pseudo-apostles from among the Jews, who had attacked him'.[5] Going on, Augustine showed that he understood very well the 'foolish discourse' of Paul in 2 Cor. 11.16-30, commenting, 'And since he was forced to praise himself, attributing this praise to a kind of folly of his own, how wisely and how eloquently he speaks!' He then quoted 2 Cor. 11.16-30, and concluded, 'Those who are awake will see how much wisdom lies in these words. With what a river of eloquence they flow even he who snores must notice'.[6] These are references to what was already a commonplace about an ideal rhetoric: an ideal rhetoric included a marriage of wisdom (*sapientia*) and eloquence (*eloquentia*).[7] Hence Augustine cited Paul's letters as examples of Christian eloquence *par excellence*: 'Surely, if we offer anything of his as an example of eloquence, we shall offer it from those Epistles which even his critics who wished to have his word seem contemptible confessed to be "weighty and strong"'.[8]

St Augustine by no means stands alone as a rhetorical critic of the New Testament. In the early nineteenth century, the German lexicographer Christian Gottlob Wilke as a rhetorical critic was primarily concerned with the investigation of the smaller rhetorical forms, particles, and sentence structure. His pedantic *Die neutestamentliche Rhetorik* concerned itself with the aesthetic form of New Testament discourses, attempting to investigate each and every 'rhetorisches Moment' ('rhetorical element').[9] Wilke did decide that Paul was 'as a writer more difficult to characterize than the remaining New Testament writers',[10] though Paul's rhetoric was described as 'clever'.[11] Interestingly enough, Wilke distinguished a rhetorical style in the 'accepted genuine' letters which was different from that of the epistles to the Ephesians and Colossians, which was also different from that of the Epistle to the Hebrews.[12] He did, however, accept both Thessalonian epistles as genuine.

The discussion of Pauline rhetoric was advanced by the article of Johannes Weiss published in 1897. Weiss began his 82-page essay, 'Beiträge zur Paulinischen Rhetorik', by stating

That Paul in his letters, which it is generally recognized he dictated and which are so expressed for public reading, laid down prominent oratorical features of the day, is not something new. The question is only how this rhetorical element should be explained and evaluated.[13]

Though Weiss rightly characterized the work in his article as 'fragmentary' and as 'suggestions', he did give an essentially positive assessment of Paul's rhetoric.

But what Paul lacks in *Kunstprosa* [art prose], he makes up for somewhat in his carefully written letters through a sure rhetorical movement, which works not without a gripping artistry, often through symmetry, rhythm, flourish, and sonority.[14]

For Weiss, an extraordinary element that made Paul's discourses oratorical was Paul's use of parallelism, which Weiss believed to be modelled on the Hebrew *parallelismus membrorum*.[15] Even though parallelism was for Paul 'only a model',[16] Weiss used it to identify patterns in a number of passages including 1 Corinthians 13.[17] Later on in the same article he attempted to determine the rhetorical structure of Romans using similar criteria.[18] At the end of the article, Weiss concluded that further work by specialists on Paul who understood Graeco-Roman rhetoric was needed.[19]

In 1898, Eduard Norden's *Die antike Kunstprosa* surveyed classical literature from the standpoint of the practical equation of rhetoric with artistic prose style.[20] This erudite scholar found Paul's rhetoric sadly lacking:

Paul is an author which I barely, with great difficulty, understand. This is clear to me for two reasons: First, his method of argumentation has a strange style; and second, his style, all things considered, is indeed unhellenic.[21]

Although Norden held that Paul's writing was not without power, especially because of his use of rhetorical devices such as repetition and antithesis,[22] his attitude towards Paul's rhetoric was basically quite negative. Two years later, Carl Friedrich Georg Heinrici countered Norden's negative judgment about Paul as a rhetorical writer with a more positive assessment in an appendix, 'Zum Hellenismus des Paulus' ('On the Hellenism of Paul'), to his commentary on 2 Corinthians.[23] Heinrici concluded that

> Paul's style is individual and gripping. Despite its various limitations, it has a unified character. No classicist, no Hellenist has written thus, and also no church father. The Hellenistic Jew overwhelmed by his Lord stands for himself. His mode of expression was not conditioned by imitation (*mimēsis*), but through the original, vivid power of his intellectual formation.[24]

Johannes Weiss's student Rudolf Bultmann wrote his doctoral dissertation comparing Pauline literature to the Cynic-Stoic diatribe, and he demonstrated several rhetorical figures in popular philosophical literature, with parallels in Pauline letters.[25]

Significant advances in the rhetorical understanding of Pauline literature were to wait some sixty years.[26] In 1968, Edwin A. Judge published a very interesting article in which he examined the question of whether Paul was indeed a 'layman in rhetoric' (*idiotēs tō logō*) as he said he was in 2 Cor. 11.6.[27] In 1961, Judge had suggested that the early Christians understood themselves as a kind of 'scholastic community',[28] and that 'Paul found himself a reluctant and unwelcomed competitor in the field of professional "sophistry" and that he promoted a deliberate collision with its standards of value'.[29] Judge argued that 'the verdict of the Fathers would be that Paul used no asteistic irony in admitting he was a layman in speech, but accepted the charge that he was in order to confound it'.[30] Like Weiss before him, Judge concluded that ' . . . we must urgently look for the scholars who will be able to give us control of the New Testament art of speech'.[31]

Those who survey what critics up to and including Judge have said about Paul's use of rhetoric will note that most of the discussion has been centered around examinations of style; and even for many contemporary classicists and New Testament scholars, there is an explicit or implicit equation of rhetoric with style and the smaller rhetorical figures. The kind of rhetorical criticism of Pauline literature that has appeared in the 1970s and since is of a markedly different sort, a rhetorical criticism no longer *primarily* concerned with the elucidation of style or the identification of smaller rhetorical figures or of a particular sentence structure. The works of Hans Dieter Betz, Wilhelm Wuellner, George A. Kennedy, Robert Jewett and others have focused on the understanding of whole documents as rhetorical discourses. Consequently their rhetorical criticism has stemmed from the identification of traditional parts of a rhetorical discourse (as taught in various ancient rhetorical handbooks) with parts of actual Pauline letters. In 1975, Hans Dieter Betz published a seminal article, 'The Literary Composition and Function of Paul's Letter to the Galatians', in which he argued that Paul wrote Galatians having in mind the standard parts of a rhetorical speech, and that rhetorical criteria should be used to interpret that letter.[32] In 1976, Wilhelm Wuellner wrote an article in which he argued that the structure of Romans followed the pattern of a rhetorical speech, followed in 1979 by another article exploring the rhetorical structure of 1 Corinthians 13.[33] Late in 1979 appeared Hans Dieter Betz's large commentary on Galatians, which was structured around his rhetorical analysis of that epistle as an 'apologetic letter'.[34] In 1982, Robert Jewett published an article, 'Romans as an Ambassadorial Letter', in which he argued that Romans is a rhetorical letter in which Paul attempted to unify the Roman house-churches so that they could support his projected mission to Spain.[35] In 1984 George A. Kennedy published *New Testament Interpretation through Rhetorical Criticism*, which was the first work to teach rhetorical criticism as a method of New Testament interpretation of both epistles and gospels. The following year Betz brought out another commentary, *2 Corinthians 8 and 9*, which used rhetorical criteria to explain many of the literary features of these letter fragments, comparing them with administrative correspondence in the Hellenistic period and other letters such as Cicero's.[36]

Michael Bünker's study of the rhetoric of 1 Corinthians integrates studies of rhetorical *dispositio* (arrangement) with epistolographic studies of Hellenistic letters.[37] He identifies various sections of the canonical 1 Corinthians with traditional parts of rhetorical speeches. The lengthy study of the argumentation of Romans 9–11 by Folker Siegert uses rhetorical precepts as found in Chaim Perelman's *New Rhetoric* to guide the analysis of that most difficult section of Romans, relating Paul's argumentation to theories of semiotics as well as rhetoric.[38] In 1984 also appeared Klaus Berger's *Formgeschichte des Neuen Testaments* which gathers New Testament literary forms under the three *genera* of rhetoric.[39] Every year sees more and more papers presented at the Annual Meeting of the Society of Biblical Literature in both the Rhetorical Criticism section and the Pauline Epistles section which use and develop rhetorical criticism of New Testament epistles. Rhetorical criticism is becoming more and more widely recognized as a method of interpretation of Pauline literature, as well as other biblical literature.[40]

The discussion of the rhetorical function of letters was also advanced by Abraham J. Malherbe's useful article, 'Ancient Epistolary Theorists', which was published in 1977.[41] In this work Malherbe collected and translated several of the ancient epistolary (letter-writing) handbooks which date from approximately the first century BCE to the sixth century CE. Malherbe stated that

> Epistolary theory in antiquity belonged to the domain of the rhetoricians, but it was not originally part of their theoretical systems. It is absent from the earliest extant rhetorical handbooks, and it only gradually made its way into the genre.[42]

Malherbe did point out, however, that 'Demetrius's' handbook *De elocutione* ('On Style'), which has been dated from the third century BCE to the first century CE, included a discussion of letters and their styles.[43] 'Demetrius' taught that, of the four conventional styles of rhetoric, the elevated style, the graceful style, the plain style, and the forcible style, letters should be written in a combination of the plain style and the graceful style. 'Demetrius' also compared letters to dialogues: a letter was in the same style as a dialogue and constituted one part of a dialogue (*De elocutione* 223). Although Malherbe never defined a clear relationship between rhetoric and letters (nor did Heikki Koskenniemi in his classic study of Greek letters[44]), nevertheless he showed that letter-writing instruction was indeed part of the conventional curriculum of grammar schools in the early empire.[45] He also pointed out that 'Cicero did know rhetorical prescriptions on letters and was probably familiar with handbooks on letter writing'.[46] Yet Cicero's comments on letter types were, according to Malherbe, '. . . not the basis for an epistolographic system, nor are they part of such a system. They are rather practical, conventional means of finding an appropriate form for important situations to which letters are addressed'.[47] On the other hand, systems of rhetoric, as we know several of them from the extant rhetorical handbooks, are sometimes not much more than 'practical, conventional means of finding an appropriate form' to meet situations of contingency in which a persuasive response is needed. In fact, Malherbe's phrase is not far distant from Aristotle's classic definition of rhetoric, 'the faculty for finding the available means of persuasion in any subject whatsoever'.[48]

Two studies of different aspects of Graeco-Roman epistolography which appeared in 1986 also inform the discussion about epistolary rhetoric. John L. White's collection, *Light from Ancient Letters*, is limited to documentary letters written on papyri, excluding Hellenistic royal correspondence and 'literary' letters.[49] On 'literary' letters, White comments, 'The use of rhetorical techniques, especially in the theological body of St. Paul's letters, indicates that a knowledge of these traditions is quite relevant to the study of early Christian letters'.[50] White mentions the 'Christian letter tradition . . . in which a Christian leader wrote a letter of instruction to a Christian community under his leadership'.[51] White sees St Paul as the creator of this tradition, when he wrote to churches he had previously founded. At the end of his collection, White gives an overview of Greek letter writing, where he considers various school traditions of letter writing and modern theories of letter writing, to some degree based on the epistolary handbook *Typoi Epistolikoi* ('Epistolary Types', dated from the third century BCE to the third century CE) falsely attributed to Demetrius of Phalerum, as well as the epistolary handbook *Epistolimaioi Charaktēres* ('Epistolary Characters', dated from the fourth to the sixth centuries CE) falsely attributed to Libanius.[52] To a certain extent following the epistolary types (and within the limits of 'nonliterary' or documentary letters), White is able to categorize some letters as 'letters of instruction and recommendation', 'letters of petition', and 'family letters'.

Especially useful are White's well-documented lists of standard epistolary formulas, including formulas in the opening and closing of the letters and formulas in the letter body. These latter formulas include disclosure formulas, such as 'Therefore I wrote you in order that you may know . . . ', similar to St. Paul's formula, 'We do not want you to be ignorant, brothers, concerning . . . '[53] Other formulas include 'statements of reassurance, concern, and other conventions', as well as various requests and instructions.[54] White's characterization of 'statements used to persuade, coerce, or threaten',[55] could be seen to impinge rather directly on theories of rhetoric, the 'art of persuasion'.

Stanley K. Stowers's book, *Letter Writing in Greco-Roman Antiquity*, is a work which seeks to understand New Testament letters by means of theories and letter types primarily found in the epistolary handbooks of Pseudo-Demetrius and Pseudo-Libanius. Stowers's work also interacts in important ways with rhetorical traditions. Essentially accepting the Aristotelian division of rhetoric into three *genera*, Stowers finds that most Graeco-Roman letter types were associated with epideictic rhetoric, whose standard topics were praise and blame.[56] He finds also that

> Two types of letters, the accusing and the apologetic, clearly fall under judicial rhetoric. The letter of advice would also clearly seem to belong to deliberative rhetoric. Most other kinds of letters could be conceived of as belonging to epideictic, which had two departments, praise and blame.[57]

Stowers argues, however, that epistolary classification 'according to the three species of rhetoric only partially works. This is because the letter-writing tradition was essentially independent of rhetoric'.[58]

A monograph on letters by Hermann Peter, *Der Brief in der römischen Literatur*, published in 1901, understood Graeco-Roman letter writing as a part of rhetorical tradition.[59] Peter argued that official letters were seen in Greek tradition as substitutes for or representations of public speeches ('letter and speech were looked upon as belonging together'[60]) and thus teaching about letters was a natural part of Graeco-Roman education, particularly within rhetorical schools. Peter argued that the systematic rules taught in rhetorical schools had a powerful influence on all kinds of speeches and also letters.[61]

There is no doubt that St Paul (and for that matter, other authors whose writings are preserved in the Pauline corpus) intended Pauline letters to be persuasive, and that what is being persuaded varies greatly from letter to letter. It is true that rhetorical rules and precepts were developed for oral discourses, but it is also not unreasonable to believe that rhetorical principles were used either directly or indirectly in the composition of letters, for several reasons. Graeco-Roman rhetoric had often affected the composition of written discourses, since Aristotle mentions a style proper to written discourses in his discussion of rhetorical styles,[62] and since Isocrates, the Athenian statesman and the most influential teacher of rhetoric in his day, was well known for the elegant literary style of his orations.[63] In the midst of discussions of rhetorical styles, Quintilian and Apollonius of Tyana mention a style appropriate to letters.[64] Most notably, Cicero in his mature work *De oratore* has one of his rhetorical heroes argue that when official messages, presumably in the form of letters, must be sent to or from the Senate and must be written in an elaborate style, no other *genus* of rhetoric (beyond the traditional three *genera*) is needed, 'since the ability acquired by a ready speaker, from the treatment of his other subjects and topics, will not fail him in situations of that description'.[65] Thus Cicero argued that (1) it is quite natural for letters written for official purposes to use rhetoric, and (2) letters could be understood as belonging to (or at least being strongly affected by) the three traditional *genera* of rhetoric. Similarly, it seems clear that Pauline letters were official and relatively public communications from Paul to various churches he had founded, since in the earliest of his extant letters, Paul ordered, 'I adjure you by the Lord to read the letter to all the brethren' (1 Thess. 5.27; cf. Col. 4.16).

Another set of connections between rhetoric and letters includes the treatments of letters in the two Hellenistic epistolary handbooks cited above. The handbook of Pseudo-Demetrius advised its readers that twenty-one epistolary types were in existence. Examination of the names of these types shows that several of the types are named with technical terminology from Graeco-Roman rhetoric, as witnessed in the rhetorical handbooks. For example, the 'blaming' (*memptikos*) type and the 'praising' (*epainetikos*) type seem to be clearly related to epideictic rhetoric because the standard topics of this *genus* of rhetoric are praise and blame. In Aristotle's *Ars rhetorica*, epideictic rhetoric is described as a *genos* of rhetoric in 1.2.3, and then in 1.3.5 and 1.3.7 the phrase 'those who praise or blame' (*tois epainousi kai psegousi; hoi epainountes kai hoi psegontes*)[66] is employed as a synonym for those who do epideictic rhetoric. The *symbouleutikos* ('advising') type of letter would seem to be related to the *genus* of rhetoric called *symbouleutikon* (deliberative).[67] Similarly, the *apologētikos* ('defensive') type of letter shares its title with one of the parts of judicial rhetoric, *apologia* or 'defense'.[68] The *psektikos* ('vituperative') letter seems to have a name in common with the *psektikon* ('vituperative') kind of rhetoric, which along with 'enkomiastic' (*egkōmiastikon*) rhetoric seems to constitute the *genus* of epideictic rhetoric in the *Rhetorica ad Alexandrum*.[69] It appears, therefore, that some of the technical terminology of rhetorical style, topics, and *genera* became part of the terminology of the relatively little we know of systematic teaching about letters.

The relation between rhetoric and letters may also be viewed from the perspective of mediaeval rhetoric. In the Middle Ages, rhetoric developed greatly in the direction of literary (as opposed to oral) discourses, although the art of preaching (*ars praedicandi*) was by no means neglected. The two most important literary *artes* were the art of verse-writing (*ars poetriae*) and the art of letter-writing (*ars dictaminis*). One of the most important contributions to the mediaeval art of letter-writing was the *Dictaminum radii* (or *Flores rhetorici*) of Alberic of Monte Cassino, a 'teacher in the oldest continuously operating Benedictine monastery in Europe', who 'inherited the ancient traditions of learning which went back to Benedict himself'.[70] In the *Dictaminum radii*, written about 1087, there is an unmistakable correlation between the use of rhetoric and written works. This work concentrated on material at the beginning of written rhetorical discourses, the *exordium* and the *captatio benevolentiae* (the acquisition of good-will), and Alberic devoted the longest treatment in this treatise to the relationship between the *salutatio* (salutation of letters) and the *exordium* (3.5-6), clearly showing that he had letters in mind, as does 'his statement that the first thing to consider is "the person to whom and the person from whom it is sent"'.[71] Alberic showed that he had the *partes orationis* in mind when he wrote, 'After the salutation [belongs] the *exordium*', and 'after the *exordium* the narration. . .'.[72] In his other work *Breviarium de dictamine*, Alberic frequently referred to letters, and it is hard to dispute James J. Murphy's conclusion 'that Alberic's school at Monte Cassino was actively engaged in discussing the nature of letters'.[73]

In an anonymous work written around 1135 and called *Rationes dictandi*, which reflects 'the basic doctrines of the *ars dictaminis*' which 'were crystallized in the region of Bologna',[74] the fourth of its thirteen sections taught that letters have five parts, namely, *salutatio*, *benevolentiae captatio*, *narratio*, *petitio*, *conclusio*. Thus it is clear that the *partes orationis* had been adapted into standard letter parts in the region of Bologna no later than the early twelfth century.[75] A wider provenance for the understanding of letters in rhetorical categories is suggested by other mediaeval and Byzantine works,[76] as well as Erasmus's *De conscribendis epistolis*, which treated letters according to the three traditional *genera* of rhetoric and according to the *partes orationis*.[77]

The fact that letter writing is so firmly established in the mediaeval appropriation of Graeco-Roman rhetoric suggests that the composition of letters may have been more than a peripheral concern in the actual practice of rhetors, particularly in the Hellenistic period. A more adequate explanation of the paucity of instruction about letters in the earliest rhetorical handbooks would center

around the fact that rhetorical tradition in the Hellenistic period
gave primary emphasis to judicial rhetoric, as opposed to deliberative
and epideictic rhetoric. By the time of Cicero, the *Rhetorica ad
Herennium*, and Quintilian, instruction in rhetorical schools concentrated on judicial rhetoric,[78] and these handbooks themselves tended
to define the other *genera* of rhetoric in terms of judicial rhetoric.
The fact that it was rhetorically undesirable to write letters, as stated
earlier in this chapter, as well as the fact that the teaching in
handbooks tended to teach about and presuppose ideal situations, as
Cicero complained,[79] made it unlikely that the rhetorical handbooks
would give much attention to letters. Yet rhetoric, particularly
deliberative rhetoric, had traditionally been centered around the
need for men to speak up for their own interests, and that of their
city, in front of political bodies which had the power to make
decisions which would affect their future. A letter, lacking the *ēthos*
and delivery of the rhetor, was considered a very poor substitute for
the rhetor's own presence, a substitution that would be made only in
the direst of straits, such as that exemplified by Demosthenes' *Epistle*
1, which we shall analyze later in this chapter. Demosthenes, Paul,
and others wrote the letters they did because, being far away from
the people they had to persuade, they had no other option. Since the
doing of crucial kinds of persuasion by letters was so undesirable, it is
unlikely that rhetorical teachers would want to make letters a part of
rhetorical theory. On the other hand, given the fact that instruction
in rhetoric was given by grammar teachers as well as rhetorical
teachers,[80] and given the fact that letters of famous persons appear to
have been a part of rhetorical instruction,[81] one can be skeptical
about an absolute separation between rhetorical instruction and
grammatical instruction, so that instruction about letters could very
well have taken place within the context of learning specific
strategies of persuasion. Although the major domain of rhetoric, in
the Hellenistic period and before it, was the spoken persuasive word,
the fact that Paul's letters could be considered 'weighty and strong'
by his most professionally competent rhetorical enemies (2 Cor.
10.10) suggests that Paul was able to make letter-writing into a fine
art. The notion that Paul might use rhetorical principles and patterns
in doing persuasion by letter does not speak against the quality of his
rhetoric; rather, it speaks strongly in favor of his rhetorical
creativity.

The publication of White's *Light from Ancient Letters*, of course, raises the issue of the multiplicity of kinds of letters to which early Christian letters can be compared. The papyus letters we have exhibit a remarkable diversity in function, if not in form. The parallels from documentary (or 'nonliterary') letters to New Testament letters, especially in the more formulaic parts of letters at their beginnings and ends, can be quite precise. John White's interesting form-critical analysis of the body of the Greek letter tells us much about certain components of Hellenistic documentary letter tradition, in terms of form and function.[82] However, epistolographic studies generally do not make it clear just how form is related to the *content* of particular letters. Form-critical studies can indeed explain *how* parts of letters are constructed (at least some of the parts), but they seem less helpful when it comes to explaining *why* certain letter formulae were used rather than others.

The question that rhetorical analysis of letters can answer, that epistolographic analysis alone does not appear to answer very well, is this: Just how are the structure and function of a letter related to its content and the intention of its writer? If this question can be answered, then scholars will be well on their way towards answering one of the most traditional questions asked by form-critics, i.e., What was the *Sitz im Leben* ('situation in life' in which the literature was composed) of the document being examined? I propose that rhetorical criticism can help scholars to identify the lived situation of letters in the Pauline corpus,[83] primarily because the use of certain rhetorical *genera* and topics seems to presuppose certain situations. If this is indeed the case, then rhetorical criticism can help us learn more not only about the language of letters, but about the intention of authors in writing them.

The Genera of Rhetoric

One of the major features of Aristotle's famous handbook, 'The Art of Rhetoric' (here referred to as *Ars rhetorica*), is its logical division of rhetoric into three 'kinds' (*eidē* or *genē*), or in Latin, *genera* (plural of *genus*). The three *genera* of rhetoric are deliberative (*symbouleutikon*), judicial (*dikanikon*), and epideictic (*epideiktikon*).[84] In Aristotle's rhetorical system, they were linked and differentiated through by the phenomenon of time.

Further, to each of these a special time is appropriate: to the deliberative the future, for the speaker, whether he exhorts or dissuades, always advises about things to come; to the forensic the past, for it is always in reference to things done that one party accuses and the other defends; to the epideictic most appropriately the present, for it is the existing condition of things that all those who praise or blame have in view. It is not uncommon, however, for epideictic speakers to avail themselves of other times, of the past by way of recalling it, or of the future by way of anticipating it.[85]

Thus, Aristotle taught here that epideictic rhetoric had to do with the past and future, as well as the present, although the proper time for deliberative rhetoric was the future and the proper time for judicial rhetoric was the past. Since Aristotle noted elsewhere that the present was also an appropriate time for deliberative rhetoric,[86] it would not be too much to say that the overlapping of subjects and topics in time became an illustration of, if not a justification for, the overlapping of the *genera* of rhetoric in Aristotle's understanding.

Judicial (or 'forensic') rhetoric dealt with defense and accusation, and its normative locus was the lawcourts. When a rhetor was either defending his client or acting as a prosecutor, the arguments in the case had to do with past actions which the accused did or did not do, as well as the overall character of the accused. One of the greatest examples of judicial rhetoric was Demosthenes's speech *De corona* ('On the Crown'), in which the orator defended himself, his deeds and words, against the attack of his enemy Aeschines.[87] Epideictic rhetoric included praise and blame of things in the present; praise was much more common than blame. Funeral speeches, such as the famous funeral speech of Pericles found in Thucydides' *History of the Peloponnesian War* 2.35, are some of the most important examples of epideictic rhetoric.[88] Deliberative rhetoric, as its Greek name *symbouleutikon* suggests, was rhetoric given before the council (*boulē*) and which argued for or against specific actions by the body politic which would affect the future for good or ill. Thus in Aristotle's view, the successful deliberative rhetor argued his case on the basis of what was expedient and/or harmful to the hearers of the speech. The related topics of honor and justice, therefore, were to be introduced in the context of what is expedient and/or harmful to the audience to whom the rhetor is speaking.

Aristotle's rhetorical system became practically canonical within the realm of rhetoric, for a variety of reasons. First, though the Aristotelian system of rhetoric was taken up and modified by Cicero in *De inventione* and Quintilian in *Institutio oratoria*, the Aristotelian system had become quite influential before Cicero,[89] partially because Aristotle's system had much in common with the earlier systematization of Isocrates.[90] Second, Aristotle's understanding of the relations among the three *genera* of rhetoric is intrinsically brilliant and logical. Judicial rhetoric really did deal with defense and accusation on the basis of deeds done in the past. Epideictic rhetoric really did deal with the praise and blame of people and things, mostly for aspects of their existence in the present, though overlapping with the past and future as well. And when a rhetor spoke before a deliberative body, the goal of the speech was generally to advise that body on making decisions which would affect that body's existence and well-being in the future. Thus, since the best guides for the future have always been the past and present, even though the *genus* of deliberative rhetoric really did deal mostly with the future, there is a necessary overlap with the past and present in this *genus* as well. Hence, Aristotle's categorization of rhetoric into the three *genera*, relating them and yet differentiating them on the basis of time, can be considered one of the most important developments in the history of rhetoric. In addition, the relating of the three *genera* by Aristotle through time is quite consistent with the universal character of rhetoric itself, as defined by Aristotle.[91]

Although it is clear that rhetoric had been practiced in each of the three *genera* of rhetoric well before Aristotle,[92] it is nonetheless true that the first 'creator of a systematic and scientific "Art" of Rhetoric is Aristotle'.[93] Moreover, the organization of rhetoric into the three *genera* of judicial, epideictic, and deliberative rhetoric became and remained an important foundation for the understanding and teaching of rhetoric well into the Middle Ages and Renaissance.

The Parts of Rhetorical Discourses (partes orationis)

The rhetorical handbooks from Graeco-Roman antiquity, beginning with Aristotle's *Ars rhetorica*, exhibit a remarkable amount of consensus concerning the standard parts of the rhetorical discourse (*partes orationis*). Aristotle wrote in *Ars rhetorica* 3.13.4, 'These divisions are appropriate to every speech, and at most the parts are four in number, *exordium* (*prooimion*), statement (*prothesis*), proof (*pistis*), and epilogue (*epilogos*)'. The statement of the case may at times include a narrative (*diēgēsis*), though Aristotle taught that this was not necessary for every speech, since a narration truly belonged to judicial rhetoric.[94] Cicero's *De inventione* taught that the parts of a discourse were six in number: *exordium, narratio, partitio, confirmatio, reprehensio*, and *conclusio*.[95] Cicero's *De partitione oratoria* taught that there were four parts of a discourse: *exordium, narratio, confirmatio* and *reprehensio* (together), and *peroratio*.[96] Quintilian listed different parts of speeches according to the different *genera* of rhetoric; according to him, judicial rhetorical discourses have these parts: *prooemium, narratio, probatio, refutatio*, and *peroratio*.[97] In deliberative rhetoric an *exordium* was not always required, though the beginning of a speech 'must have some resemblance to an *exordium*'.[98] However, appeals to the emotions were required in deliberative rhetoric, probably referring to the content of the *peroratio*.[99] We may assume that a proof was required, since it is absurd to have a rhetorical discourse without a proof, either confirmatory or refutational. A *narratio* was not required in deliberative rhetoric, but one might frequently be introduced.[100] In 4.Pr.6, Quintilian set forth his program for books 4-6, namely the explication of the *prooemium*, the *narratio*, the *probatio* (either confirmatory or refutational), and the *peroratio*, although his actual discussion included the *exordium* (4.1), the *narratio* (4.2), the *propositio* (4.4), the *partitio* (4.5), proofs (5), and the *peroratio* (6.1).

The *Rhetorica ad Herennium*, which seems to come from the early first century BCE, also taught about various parts of the rhetorical discourse: *exordium, narratio, divisio, confirmatio, confutatio, conclusio*.[101] As late as the sixth century CE, Boethius wrote: 'This rhetorical discourse has six parts, the prooemium, which is the *exordium*, the narrative, the partition, the confirmation, the refutation, the peroration; and these are the parts of the instrument of the rhetorical discipline'.[102]

Thus in the above rhetorical handbooks which date from the fourth century BCE to the sixth century CE, one can see a large amount of consensus, as represented in the following table:[103]

Greek	Latin
prooimion	exordium
diēgēsis	narratio

prothesis, *et al.*	partitio, propositio
pistis	probatio, often divided into
	confirmatio and reprehensio
epilogos	peroratio.

The best explanation of the similarities and differences among the various rhetorical handbooks is the living tradition of rhetoric itself, which included a variety of understandings of what rhetoric was, whether it was a good thing or a bad thing, or whether it was something quite neutral which could be used in different ways; what the purposes of rhetoric were; how one went about learning and teaching rhetoric; whether rhetoric was primarily an oral or a literary phenomenon; and whether or not it was an honorable thing to persuade people by aiming at their emotions. In the light of the complexity of this intellectual and practical tradition which predates Socrates and stretches into the Middle Ages and Renaissance, the consensus as to what the *partes orationis* are and do is quite striking.[104]

Assuming that this consensus reflects an ongoing tradition of teaching about how speeches should be put together (*dispositio*), it should be possible to analyze rhetorical discourses according to precisely these categories, if the parts of the discourses do really seem to do what the handbooks say they should do. In other words, since there is wide agreement in the extant handbooks (several of which are based on older handbooks no longer extant), it should be possible to do rhetorical criticism on discourses based on the precepts of these handbooks. Hence this study will proceed by summarizing the consensus in the extant handbooks as to the nature and functions of the *partes*, and then it will attempt to show how 2 Thessalonians can be interpreted according to the rhetorical significance of its *partes*.

The Exordium. The rhetorical handbooks agree that the rhetorical discourse has an introduction which is called *prooimion* in Greek or *prooemium* or *exordium* in Latin. Aristotle wrote:

> The exordium [*prooimion*] is the beginning of a speech, as the prologue [*prologos*] in poetry and the prelude in flute-playing: for all these are beginnings, and as it were a paving the way for what follows.[105]

The *exordium* of discourses did exactly that: it introduced the rhetor and his subject to the audience. In epideictic rhetoric, Aristotle says, the *exordia* derive from the topics of blame and praise.[106] Judicial rhetoric's *exordia*, according to Aristotle,

> provide a sample of the subject, in order that the hearers may know beforehand what it is about . . . so then he who puts the beginning, so to say, into the hearer's hand enables him, if he holds fast to it, to follow the story . . . So then the most essential and special function of the exordium is to make clear what is the end or purpose of the speech.[107]

However, Aristotle recognized that other reasons for *exordia* included the weaknesses of the audience.[108] These other forms of *exordia* are 'remedies' for such weaknesses of the audience.[109] The most important type of 'remedy'-*exordium* is the appeal to the audience. For this, then,

> The reason is obvious. The defendant, when about to introduce himself, must remove all obstacles, so that he must first clear away all prejudices; the accuser must create prejudice in the epilogue, that his hearers may have a livelier recollection of it. The object of an appeal to the hearer is to make him well disposed or to arouse his indignation, and sometimes to engage his attention or the opposite. . .[110]

Aristotle quoted Homer to end his discussion of *exordia* in judicial rhetoric:

> And since it is rightly said, 'Grant that on reaching the Phaeacians I may find friendship or compassion', the orator should aim at exciting these two feelings.[111]

In Aristotle's system, deliberative rhetoric 'borrows its exordia from judicial', though Aristotle said *exordia* are 'uncommon' in deliberative rhetoric, since in this *genus* of rhetoric the hearers should be familiar with its subject. Thus, the task of deliberative rhetoric is to 'excite or remove prejudice, and to magnify or minimize the importance of the subject'.[112] According to Aristotle, the task of the epideictic orator is to 'make the hearer believe that he shares the praise, either himself, or his family, or his pursuits, or at any rate in some way or other'.[113]

Cicero's *De inventione* 1.20 gives rules for *exordia*:

> An *exordium* is a passage which brings the mind of the auditor into a proper condition to receive the rest of the speech. This will be

accomplished if he [the auditor] becomes well-disposed, attentive, and receptive.[114]

Further instruction by Cicero on the *exordium* takes the form of audience psychology, that is, how to make the audience well-disposed towards the orator, given the mood the audience is in and the nature of the case.[115] Conversely, of an *exordium* which does not perform these functions, Cicero says, 'nothing surely can be worse than that'.[116]

Quintilian deals with the *exordium* in 4.1 of his *Institutio oratoria*. Its optimal definition included the notion that this section of a discourse 'is designed as an introduction to the subject on which the orator has to speak'.[117] The 'sole purpose' of the *exordium* for Quintilian, like the young Cicero, 'is to prepare our audience in such a way that they will be disposed to lend a ready ear to the rest of the speech'.[118] Much of the rest of Quintilian's treatment of the *exordium* agrees with the treatment by the young Cicero in *De inventione*, especially the notion that the orator goes about making his audience 'well-disposed, attentive, and ready to receive instruction' (*si benevolum, attentum, docilem fecerimus*).[119]

The Narratio. Aristotle gave guidance concerning the *diēgēsis* (*narratio* in Latin) in *Ars rhetorica* 3.16, based on the needs of each of the three *genera* of rhetoric. 'In the epideictic style the narrative should not be consecutive, but disjointed'.[120] In defense (a part of judicial rhetoric), 'the narrative need not be so long, for the points at issue are either that the fact has not happened or that it was neither injurious nor wrong nor so important as asserted . . . '[121] The narrative 'should be of a moral character' if the subject admits of a moral end.[122] The narrative might also 'draw upon what is emotional by the introduction of such of its accompaniments as are well known, and of what is specially characteristic of either yourself or of the adversary'.[123] In the narrative, the rhetor may also introduce himself and his adversary as being 'of a certain moral character'.[124] However, in deliberative rhetoric, 'narrative is very rare, because no one can narrate things to come'.[125] This clearly relates to Aristotle's understanding of the proper times of each of the *genera* of rhetoric. Deliberative rhetoric deals properly with the future, since the rhetor, 'whether he exhorts or dissuades, always advises about things to come'.[126] Judicial rhetoric was proper to the discussion of the past, 'for it is always in reference to things done that one party accuses and the other defends'. Epideictic rhetoric appertains 'most appropriately to the present, for it is the existing condition of things that all those who praise or blame have in view. It is not uncommon, however, for epideictic speakers to avail themselves of other times, of the past by way of recalling it, or of the future by way of anticipating it'.[127] Thus according to Aristotle's system, a deliberative discourse is unlikely to have a *narratio*.

Cicero in *De inventione* 1.27 gave rules for the *narratio*: 'The narrative is an exposition of events that have occurred or are supposed to have occurred'. Cicero distinguished three kinds of *narrationes*:

> one which contains just the case and the whole reason for the dispute; a second in which a digression is made beyond the strict limits of the case for the purpose of attacking somebody, or of making a comparison, or of amusing the audience in a way not incongruous with the business at hand, or for amplification. The third kind is wholly unconnected with public issues, which is recited or written solely for amusement but at the same time provides valuable training.[128]

The three important characteristics of the *narratio* of whatever type are that it should be 'brief, clear, and plausible' (*ut brevis, ut aperta, ut probabilis sit*).[129] With regard to brevity, Cicero advised orators to begin with what needs to be said but not to burden the reader or listener with useless details.[130] Clarity is to be achieved in a *narratio* 'if the events are presented one after another as they occurred, and the order of events in time is preserved so that the story is told as it will prove to have happened or will seem possible to have happened'.[131] Plausibility will be achieved in the *narratio* 'if it seems to embody characteristics which are accustomed to appear in real life'.[132] In addition to this, Cicero advises, 'one must also be on guard not to insert a narrative when it will be a hindrance or of no advantage'.[133] Thus, a *narratio* 'is also useless when the audience has grasped the facts so thoroughly that it is of no advantage to us to instruct them in a different fashion. In such a case one must dispense with narrative altogether'.[134]

Quintilian dealt with the *narratio* in *Institutio oratoria* 4.2. He taught that the *narratio* is not indispensable, since some *causae* were so brief as to require 'only a brief summary rather than a full statement of the facts'.[135] Also, some *causae* did not require a *narratio*

38   *Early Christian Rhetoric and 2 Thessalonians*

as they are 'well known to the judge or have been correctly set forth by a previous speaker'.[136] Quintilian did advise that the *narratio*, when there was one, should follow immediately upon the *exordium*, unless there was some special reason for not doing so.[137] Quintilian defined the *narratio* in 4.2.31: 'The statement of facts [*narratio*] consists in the persuasive exposition of that which either has been done, or is supposed to have been done. . .' On the nature of the *narratio*, Quintilian referred to earlier traditions: 'Most writers, more especially those of the Isocratean school, hold that it should be lucid, brief, and plausible [*lucidam, brevem, verisimilem*] (for it is of no importance if we substitute clear [*perspicuam*] for lucid, or credible or plausible [*probabilem credibilemve*]). I agree with this classification of its qualities. . .'[138] Hence, Quintilian was in essential agreement here with Cicero's *De inventione*, especially in the ways that one causes the *narratio* to have these qualities,[139] although Quintilian's treatment is much more fulsome than Cicero's. The *Rhetorica ad Herennium* in dealing with *narratio* had a categorization into three types of *narrationes* similar to that in *De inventione* 1.27 quoted above, in *Rhetorica ad Herennium* 1.12. Also, a *narratio* should have three properties: brevity, clarity, and plausibility (*ut brevis, ut dilucida, ut veri similis sit*),[140] as *De inventione* and Quintilian also advised. The discussion of *narratio* here is also based on the exposition of how to get these three qualities in the *narratio*, in 1.14-16. Hence, the *Rhetorica ad Herennium* correctly concluded: 'In what I have thus far said I believe that I agree with the other writers on the art of rhetoric. . .'[141]

The Partitio. There is no single equivalent to *partitio* in Greek rhetoric, but several terms such as *prothesis, prokataskeuē, peribolē, proekthesis*, and *hyposchesis* seem to be the Greek equivalents of the *partitio*, which is also known as the *propositio*.[142] In *De inventione* 1.31-34, Cicero discusses the *partitio*. In his understanding the *partitio* takes two forms (*partes*).[143] In both forms the goal is to make the *causa* clear and to help determine the nature of the controversy. The first form is a statement of agreements and disagreements with the opponents; 'as a result of this some definite problem is set for the auditor on which he ought to have his attention fixed'. In the second form of *partitio*,

> the matters which we intend to discuss are briefly set forth in a methodical way. This leads the auditor to hold definite points in his

mind, and to understand that when these have been discussed the oration will be over.[144]

The first form of *partitio*, namely the statement of agreement and disagreement with opponents, 'should', in Cicero's words, 'turn the subject of agreement to the advantage of the speaker's case'.[145] The second form of *partitio*, that which contains an *expositio* of topics to be discussed, ought to have three qualities: 'brevity, completeness, and conciseness' [*brevitas, absolutio, paucitas*].[146] These qualities then became the subject of discussion in 1.32-33. Brevity was defined as the use of no unnecessary word. Completeness in the *partitio* meant that everything that is argued in the discourse was mentioned in the *partitio*.[147] Conciseness in the *partitio* meant not confusing *genus* with *species*, as well as only mentioning *genera*.[148]

Quintilian discussed the *partitio* in *Institutio oratoria* 4.5, in which he defined it as the enumeration in order of *propositiones*.[149] The *propositio* as discussed in 4.4 seems to constitute the beginning of each proof. Its goal was to state what the question to be decided is. This may include a statement of agreements and disagreements with opponents. Thus the *partitio*, as discussed in 4.5, 'will, if judiciously employed, greatly add to the lucidity and grace of the speech [*lucis et gratiae confert*]'.[150] It did this by 'isolating the points from the crowd in which they would otherwise be lost and placing them before the eyes of the judge' and by setting limits on the arguments so that the listener or reader can be aware of what part of the argument has been completed.[151] Thus *propositiones*, whether they are single or multiple, must first be 'clear and lucid [*aperta atque lucida*]'. Second, 'it must be brief [*brevis*] and contain no unnecessary word'.[152] Redundancy was to be avoided by not confusing *genus* and *species* and thus not enumerating *species* which are part of a *genus* mentioned.[153] Quintilian's treatment is very much in agreement with the treatment in Cicero's *De inventione* 1.32 as discussed above.

The *Rhetorica ad Herennium*, also like Cicero, understood that the *partitio* (which it calls the *divisio*) had two *partes*.[154] The first *pars* included a statement of agreements and disagreements with opponents, and the second *pars* (called *distributio*) included enumeration and exposition of the points which would be discussed in the *probatio*. Cicero in *De inventione* had understood these two *partes* as different forms of the *partitio*; the *Rhetorica ad Herennium* seems to understand that each *divisio* included both *partes*.[155] Nevertheless, the *divisio* in the *Rhetorica ad Herennium* seems to based on the *partitio* found elsewhere in Latin rhetoric. Indeed, the *Rhetorica ad Herennium* taught that the exposition 'consists in setting forth briefly and completely [*breviter et absolute*], the points we intend to discuss';[156] as compared with 'brevity, completeness, conciseness' [*brevitas, absolutio, paucitas*] in *De inventione* 1.32.

The Probatio. The proof (Greek *pistis*; Latin *probatio* or *confirmatio / reprehensio* [or *refutatio*]) is considered the most important part of the rhetorical discourse, truly its *sine qua non*. The proof is the core of the discourse; everything that goes before it leads up to it, and the *peroratio* serves to underscore it.

Without a proof there simply is no rhetorical discourse, since nothing has been persuaded. Aristotle's *Ars rhetorica* 3.13.4 says, 'So then the necessary parts of a speech are the statement of the case and the proof. These divisions are appropriate to every speech, and at most the parts are four in number—exordium, statement, proof, epilogue'. Aristotle includes refutation and comparison as part of the proof, since both refutation and comparison prove something.[157] Methods which may be employed in the proofs are discussed in 3.17.3–18.7. Amplification is especially appropriate for epideictic speeches, 'as a rule, to prove that things are honorable or useful'.[158] Deliberative rhetoric may be characterized by arguments 'that certain consequences will not happen, or that what the adversary recommends will happen, but that it will be unjust, inexpedient, or not so important as supposed'.[159] Examples (*paradeigmata*) according to 3.17.5, were 'best suited to deliberative oratory and enthymemes to judicial. The first [deliberative] is concerned with the future, so that its examples must be derived from the past; the second [judicial] with the question of the existence or non-existence of facts, in which demonstrative and necessary proofs are more in place; for the past involves a kind of necessity'.[160]

Cicero in *De inventione* divided the proof into two parts, the *confirmatio* and the *reprehensio*. *Confirmatio* was defined as the 'part of the oration which by marshalling arguments lends credit, authority, and support to our case'.[161] The *reprehensio* was

> that part of an oration in which arguments are used to impair, disprove, or weaken the confirmation or proof in our opponents' speech. It utilizes the same sources of invention that confirmation does, because any proposition can be attacked by the same methods of reasoning by which it can be supported... Therefore the rules

for the invention and embellishment of arguments may properly be
transferred from what has been said before to this part of the
oration.[162]

Quintilian in *Institutio oratoria* devoted essentially all of book 5 to
proofs. For Quintilian, the proof was the most important part of the
discourse, since 'there can be no suit in which the proof is not
absolutely necessary'.[163] Hence, Cicero and Quintilian agree on the
existence of this part and its place within the structure of the
speech.

The same is true of the *Rhetorica ad Herennium*, which reads,
'The entire hope of victory and the entire method of persuasion rest
on proof and refutation, for when we have submitted our arguments
and destroyed those of the opposition, we have, of course, completely
fulfilled the speaker's function'.[164] Differing kinds of proofs and
refutations were advised for the different *genera* of rhetoric, based on
the topics that are to be discussed. For example, the proofs in
deliberative rhetoric were discussed in 3.8; since the end of
deliberative rhetoric, according to *Rhetorica ad Herennium*, is
advantage (which had the two subdivisions of the consideration of
security and the consideration of honor), the proofs in deliberative
rhetoric were properly based on these two topics, which can be
further subdivided. Thus in deliberative rhetoric the proof and
refutation 'establish in our favour the topics explained above, and
refute the contrary topics'.[165] Consequently the proof and refutation
according to the *Rhetorica ad Herennium* served the same basic
purposes as the proof and refutation according to other rhetorical
handbooks.

The Peroratio. The *peroratio* (Greek *epilogos*) forms the end of
rhetorical discourses, hence the term for it in the *Rhetorica ad
Herennium*, the *conclusio*.[166] Aristotle said that the *epilogos* is the last
of the four parts of the discourse,[167] and that it has four functions: 'to
dispose the hearer favourably towards oneself and unfavourably
towards the adversary; to amplify and to deprecate; to excite the
emotions of the hearer; to recapitulate'.[168] Aristotle goes on to give
the general reason for the *epilogos* and its placement at the end of the
discourse: 'For after you have proved that you are truthful and that
the adversary is false, the natural order of things is to praise
ourselves, blame him, and put the finishing touches'.[169] In disposing
the audience favorably to one's case (and unfavorably towards that of

one's adversary, if there is one), Aristotle advised, 'One or two things should be aimed at, to show that you are either relatively or absolutely good and the adversary either relatively or absolutely bad'.[170] The excitement of the emotions of the audience was fairly self-explanatory. By way of recapitulation, the *epilogos* should give a summary statement of the proofs.[171]

Cicero defined the *peroratio* as the 'end and conclusion of the whole speech'.[172] The *peroratio* had three parts: the 'summing-up' (*enumeratio*), the 'exciting of indignation [against the enemy]' (*indignatio*), and the 'arousal of pity and sympathy' (*conquestio*). The *enumeratio*, according to Cicero, 'is a passage in which matters which have been discussed in different places here and there throughout the speech are brought together in one place and arranged so as to be seen at a glance in order to refresh the memory of the audience'.[173] The *indignatio* 'is a passage which results in arousing great hatred against some person, or violent offense at some action'.[174] The skilled rhetor had numerous means at his disposal for *indignatio*, including 'all the attributes of persons or things ... or any method of arousing enmity'.[175] The opposite of the arousal of sympathy against the adversary was the arousal of sympathy in favor of one's own argument or person, the *conquestio*. This was done, according to *De inventione*, by the use of sixteen *loci* (in Greek, *topoi*) or 'common-places' which relate to the worthiness of one's case and the person of the defendant and which seek to arouse feelings of mercy from the audience.[176]

Quintilian's treatment of the *peroratio* is found in book 6. Clearly drawing on earlier rhetorical traditions, Quintilian divided the *peroratio* ('which some call the completion [*cumulum*] and others the conclusion [*conclusio*]'[177]) into two types, 'for it may deal either with facts or with the emotional aspects of the case'.[178] *Enumeratio* was defined as the 'repetition and grouping of the facts, which the Greeks call *anakephalaiōsis* [i.e., recapitulation]'.[179] The appeal to the emotions may be employed by either defendant or plaintiff, though these would naturally appeal to different emotions.[180] Quintilian summed up his long treatment of *peroratio* as follows:

It is therefore the duty of both parties to seek to win the judge's goodwill and to divert it from their opponent, as also to excite or assuage his emotions. And the following brief rule may be laid down for the observation of both parties, that the orator should display the full strength of his case before the eyes of his judge, and, when he has made up his mind what points in his case actually deserve or may seem to deserve to excite envy, goodwill, dislike or pity, should dwell on those points by which he himself would be most moved were he trying the case.[181]

The *Rhetorica ad Herennium* referred to the *peroratio* as the *conclusio*. It was equated by this author to the Greek *epilogos*, and it consisted of three parts, 'the summing up, amplification, and appeal to pity' [*enumeratione, amplificatione, et commiseratione*].[182] The *enumeratio* here was equivalent to the *enumeratio* according to Quintilian.[183] *Amplificatio* was 'the principle of using Commonplaces to stir the hearers'.[184] The *Rhetorica ad Herennium* lists ten commonplaces that could be used for this. *Commiseratio* was the stirring up of pity in the audience.[185] Like Cicero,[186] the author of *Rhetorica ad Herennium* advised that the appeal to pity must be brief, 'for nothing dries more quickly than a tear'.[187]

In summary, it is evident that there is a wide consensus between Aristotle and extant Latin handbooks as to what the *partes orationis* were and what they did in and for the discourse. The *exordium* introduced the rhetor to the audience and may state the *causa*. The *narratio*, if there was one, stated the facts in the case. The *partitio*, if there was one, could either state the agreements and disagreements with the adversary or could list (or allude to) the arguments to be made in the proof. The *probatio* proved the case and might refute the adversary, if there was one. The *peroratio* summed up the arguments and amplified them, and it frequently excited the emotions of the audience either for one's case or against one's adversary's case, or both.

Traditions of Deliberative Rhetoric

Aristotle's *Ars rhetorica* seems most classically Aristotelian in that it defined the *genera* of rhetoric in terms of three *teloi*, as Grimaldi has pointed out,[188] but in fact Aristotle's *teloi* of each *genus* of rhetoric were actually equivalent to the topics that were traditionally associated with them. Hence the *teloi* of deliberative rhetoric included 'the expedient or harmful', which were positive and negative forms of the topic of advantage, that is, the advantageous and the disadvantageous. With regard to other traditional topics of deliberative rhetoric, such as the topics of honor and justice,

Aristotle advised that they were 'included as accessory' to the topics of the expedient and the harmful.[189] Thus Aristotle's system of rhetoric included a ranking of topics, with honor and justice understood as subsidiary topics of the topic of advantage, which implied that the rhetor introduced the topic of honor not separately from the topic of advantage, but *in terms of* the topic of advantage. In other words, the rhetor advised the *boulē* which he addresses that they should do the honorable thing because it is advantageous to be honorable. For all practical purposes, then, honor was identified with one's reputation, in Aristotle's system of rhetoric.[190]

Aristotle's interaction with rhetoric, however, was not confined to the rather late treatise *Ars rhetorica*. Early in his life he had written a collection of opinions about rhetoric by rhetoricians, entitled *Synagōgē technōn*, a 'gathering together of "arts" [of rhetoric]'.[191] Tradition has it that one of the rhetorical works included by Aristotle in his now-lost *Synagōgē technōn* was the *technē* of Isocrates. George Kennedy has argued that the fragments of Isocrates's *technē* we now have do not conform to the well-developed style of Isocrates, but that they may be genuinely Isocratean by virtue of having come from the summary of Isocrates' teaching in *Synagōgē technōn*, and that information about Isocrates' teaching could have come through oral tradition or through an internal document in his school.[192] Interestingly enough, Plutarch tells us that Demosthenes learned Isocrates' *technē* secretly,[193] and one must agree with Kennedy that this 'puzzling story can perhaps best be explained if knowledge of this handbook was not supposed to exist outside of the school'.[194] Cicero in *De inventione* 2.7 tells us of Isocrates, 'there is known to be a text book from his hand, but I have not seen it', and the fifth-century CE rhetorician Syrianus referred to Isocrates's 'private' handbook,[195] so the theory of a private handbook of Isocrates has much to commend it. Thus, one must agree with Kennedy that Isocrates' handbook 'shows that the contents of rhetorical theory were gradually expanding with the addition of material on style and on kinds of speeches, and it shows something about the state of sophistic rhetoric at the time Aristotle turned his attention to the subject'.[196]

Isocrates' *De pace* ('On the Peace'), probably written about 355 BCE, is an excellent example of deliberative rhetoric. In it, Isocrates argued for an end to the Second Social War, seeking not a union of all the Hellenes, as he had earlier in his career, but rather, 'It is enough for Isocrates now to urge Athens to set her own house in order and to take the lead in a consistent policy of peace, resorting to war only to defend the principle that the states of Hellas have the right to be free'.[197] And on what basis did Isocrates argue for peace? Isocrates employed the two topics of advantage and honor, which in this speech constantly flow together.

Isocrates argued in *De pace* 18-21 that the Athenians should make peace rather than war because (1) it was to the advantage of the Athenians to end the war, based on considerations of finance and freedom to pursue peacetime occupations, including farming and maritime trade, and (2) it was to the advantage of the Athenians to end the war because they would enjoy greater security because the Athenians' allies would be more disposed towards true friendship. We can see that the primary topic used is the topic of advantage, and that the topic of honor is subsidiary to the topic of advantage, primarily because to be honorable is to enjoy the blessings of a good reputation. At the end of *De pace*, Isocrates concluded:

> If, then, you will abide by the advice which I have given you, and if, besides, you will prove yourselves warlike by training and preparing for war but peaceful by doing nothing contrary to justice, you will render not only this city but all the Hellenes happy and prosperous ... But no matter what course the rest may take, our own position will be honourable and advantageous...

A more telling indication of deliberative rhetoric could hardly be found than the final words of Isocrates just quoted: *kalos hexei kai sympherontos*, a clear use of what were or would become the standard topics of deliberative rhetoric, honor and advantage.

A more famous political speech than the foregoing is Isocrates's *Panegyricus*, which Isocrates delivered in the autumn of 380 BCE. Not accidentally, this speech argued in favor of war, along exactly the same lines that *De pace* had argued against war, the topics of advantage and honor.

After Isocrates, the most notable practitioner of deliberative rhetoric was Demosthenes, who was born in Athens in 384 BCE. He studied rhetoric with Isaeus, who had studied with Isocrates. The course of Demosthenes' early development as an orator is the subject of many interesting stories, to be found in plenty in Plutarch's *Life of Demosthenes*. His earliest speeches were those of his prosecution of his guardians, *Against Aphobus I* and *II*, which date from 363 BCE, Demosthenes' twenty-first year. Although he won his patrimony in court, little of it remained by the time he obtained it, and so Demosthenes became a *logographos*, a speech-writer. Although Demosthenes' most famous single work is probably *De corona* ('On the Crown') a brilliant judicial speech in which he defended his life and public career, Demosthenes is best known as the rhetor who mobilized Athens against Philip II of Macedon through his deliberative speeches before the Athenian council, such as his several *Philippic* and *Olynthiac* speeches, as well as lesser-known speeches such as *On the Symmories*, *For the People of Megalopolis*, *For the Liberty of the Rhodians*, *On the Peace*, and *On the Chersonese*. A number of letters bearing Demosthenes' name survive; not all of them have equal claim to authenticity, but Jonathan A. Goldstein has demonstrated the authenticity of and provided a rhetorical analysis of several of them.[198] Whether are not any of them are authentic, it is clear that they demonstrate the use of rhetorical techniques in letters associated with the most famous deliberative rhetor in history.

Demosthenes' *First Philippic* was written in about 351-340 BCE. Kennedy noted that the major focus of the *First Philippic* was the argument on the basis of advantage; honor and justice do not seem to enter into this speech.

> It is assumed that Philip acts in his own interest, and Athens must act in hers. . . . Demosthenes so focuses Athenian interests that the question seems not one of advantage, but of necessity, not the choice of a course of action, but the pursuit of the only possibility. . . . All other rhetorical arguments are only accessory: Athens' failure to act will bring on her the deepest disgrace and will allow Philip to go unpunished, but no honor is promised Athens for action, and disinterested justice is not involved.[199]

The *Third Philippic* was one of Demosthenes' most successful deliberative speeches. Much like the *First Philippic*, the argument from advantage or expediency is used almost exclusively. The advantage that was offered to the Athenians was, of course, of no small import: it was nothing less than the salvation of the Athenians from the hands of Philip. Demosthenes in paragraphs 63-69 of this speech used the *exempla* of other cities which Philip had ravaged, a standard feature in deliberative rhetoric, but the reason these negative examples were used is that they were examples of people who acted unwisely towards Philip, to their own disadvantage. Instead of being honored citizens of their own *polis*, they had become slaves, in Demosthenes' view. By the somewhat indirect reference to the social status of the captive subjects of Philip, it is clear that the topic of honor does enter into this argument, although it seems secondary to the topic of advantage. Nevertheless, the two arguments work together powerfully in a number of Demosthenes' deliberative speeches, because it was dishonorable to choose not to fight Philip (given the kind of person he was), and more importantly, it was to the Athenians' great disadvantage not to acknowledge the reality of their conflict with Philip, especially when an early entrance into a war with Philip would have given the Athenians a better chance of protecting Athens from him. Kennedy has shown that the confluence of the arguments from advantage and honor is a standard feature of fourth-century deliberative oratory,[200] and it is easy for us to see why this was the case, after having understood the classification of rhetoric by Aristotle. Aristotle taught, as far as we know for the first time, that the distinctions between the genera of rhetoric could be understood on the basis of time. In deliberative rhetoric, a deliberative body (or a deliberative person) is asked to make a decision that will affect the future for good or ill. Hence, the arguments which have always been most effective in deliberative rhetoric are those arguments which showed that the hearers' or readers' own personal advantage (which would be realized in the future) would be affected by the decision that they must make, either by doing something or by not doing anything.

A Deliberative Rhetorical Letter: Demosthenes' Epistle 1

Perhaps the best proof of the use of rhetoric in ancient letters is not statements about letters in the various rhetorical handbooks, or even epistolary handbooks, but actual letters written by prominent rhetors. Among letters written by Greek rhetors, one should not overlook the letters of Demosthenes, who was known as the greatest Greek orator, as well as the greatest deliberative rhetor, and who was clearly one of Cicero's rhetorical heroes.[201] Goldstein showed that Demosthenes' *Epistle* 1 was conceived and executed in the style of deliberative rhetoric.[202]

In *Epistle* 1, 'On Concord', the exiled Demosthenes began with a prayer for divine inspiration for writer and readers, followed by the

A Rhetorical Summary of Demosthenes' Epistle 1

1-4	I.	Exordium	
1		A.	Invocation

        1. Reason for invocation: propriety
        2. Deities invoked: 'all the gods and goddesses'
        3. Purpose of invocation: 'that what is best for the democracy of the Athenians and for those who bear goodwill toward the democracy . . . I may be moved to write and the members of the assembly to adopt'

2   B. Epistolary prescript
        1. Superscriptio: 'Demosthenes'
        2. Adscriptio: 'to the Council and people'
        3. Salutatio: 'greetings'

2-4   C. Material concerning the relationship between Demosthenes and the Athenians
        1. First part (not discussed directly): 'the question of my return'

3   2. Second part: advantage for the Athenians
            (a) Aspects of advantage
                (i) 'glory'
                (ii) 'security'
                (iii) 'liberty'
            (b) Recipients of advantage
                (i) 'not only for you' (= the Athenians)
                (ii) 'but for all the rest of the Greeks'
        3. Third part: on the Athenians' making of decisions
            (a) Stated positively: 'provided you adopt the necessary measures'
            (b) Stated negatively: 'if you fail to recognize it or are misled'

3-4   D. The *causa* (reason) for this letter
        1. Stated in terms of the rhetor: 'I felt I had to put before the public my opinion'
        2. Digression on the difficulties of communicating by letters

4   3. Stated in terms of the need of the Athenians

5-7   II. Partitio

5   A. Topic of second proof: on establishing concord
          B. Topic of third proof: on the carrying out of decisions when passed

6   C. Topic of first proof: on not harboring grudges

7-12   III. Probatio

7   A. First proof: on not harboring grudges
        1. Statement of thesis
            (a) Negatively: the fear of bitterness makes collaborators

		(b)	Positively: those unafraid of bitterness will be tractable
	2.	First argument: public proclamation of not harboring grudges not advantageous
	3.	Second argument: actual practice of not harboring grudges will determine future expectations
8-10	B.	Second proof: on concord
8	1.	Statement of thesis
		(a) Negatively: 'you must not cast any blame'
		(b) Positively: 'you must grant that everyone has done his duty'
9	2.	First argument: on the basis of honor
9	3.	Second argument: on the basis of advantage
10	4.	Third argument: on the basis of Demosthenes' personal experience
11-12	C.	Third proof: on the carrying out of decisions when passed
11	1.	Reference to previous communication from Demosthenes on preparatory steps
11-12	2.	Statement of thesis: the carrying out of war commands are the tasks of commanding generals
12	3.	First argument: those who give advice to you are put in a difficult position
	4.	Second argument: plans carefully thought out can be spoiled when not implemented correctly
13	III. Peroratio
	A.	Transition from previous heading (*e contrario*): 'This time I hope that everything will go well'
	B.	The *exemplum* of Alexander
	1.	Statement of *exemplum*
	2.	Consequences of *exemplum*
		(a) First consequence: Alexander succeeding by activity, not by inactivity
		(b) Second consequence: Fortune is now seeking someone to accompany
14-16	IV. Exhortation
14	A.	Concerning commanders
15	B.	Concerning changes of mind (cf. second proof above)
16	C.	Concerning religious duties
	D.	Final exhortation: 'liberate the Greeks!'
16	V.	Epistolary postscript: 'Farewell'

epistolary prescript. In the *exordium* of this letter, Demosthenes only briefly mentioned the topic of his exile, passing over this topic in order to mention the two topics dealt with in the proof, the advantage of the Athenians, and the importance of making decisions and following them consistently. The two-part proof is then followed by a *peroratio*, which in turn is followed by an exhortation. Although 'exhortation' is not a traditional *pars orationis*, according to the handbooks, the presence of exhortations at the end of deliberative orations is consistent with the discussions of deliberative rhetoric in certain rhetorical handbooks, in which the prime task of the deliberative rhetor is exhortation.[203] For facility of study and discussion, we include a brief rhetorical analysis of Demosthenes' *Epistle* 1, showing the *partes orationis* of this letter in outline form.

Conclusions

From the above analysis of Demosthenes' interesting deliberative letter, a letter in which Demosthenes advised the Athenians that they should make a change in public policy that would affect their future, one can see that the *partes orationis* do function in this letter in ways that one would expect from reading about the *partes orationis* in the rhetorical handbooks. There is a clear connection between the *exordium*, the two-part proof, and the *peroratio*, and one could argue that there is also recapitulation of the second proof in the exhortation section, although recapitulation of the first proof seems to be absent. All of the *partes orationis* which are found in Demosthenes' *Epistle* 1, as well as other letters,[204] are indeed found in the Second Letter to the Thessalonians.

Just as the identification and exposition of the *partes* of Demosthenes' letter are central to the understanding of what and how the writer intended to persuade, I shall show that the identification and exposition of the *partes* of 2 Thessalonians are likewise central to the understanding of the rhetoric of this most enigmatic letter. In the following chapter of this study, I shall identify and discuss the *partes* of 2 Thessalonians and their rhetorical functions in the letter.

Chapter 3

A RHETORICAL INTERPRETATION OF 2 THESSALONIANS

The Rhetorical Structure of 2 Thessalonians

It was shown in the previous chapter of this study that rhetorical discourses in the Graeco-Roman world routinely followed the patterns set down in the major rhetorical handbooks from that period, especially the patterns concerning the standard parts and topics of speeches; and it was argued that the use of these originally oral rules is also visible in written discourses as well,[1] such as Demosthenes' *Epistle* 1. The present chapter applies rhetorical criticism, based on Graeco-Roman rhetorical traditions, to the text of 2 Thessalonians.

1.1-12, the exordium. The major tasks of any *exordium* are to introduce the rhetor to his audience and to gain their goodwill. In ancient Greek letters in the Hellenistic period, this was done in a standard way which contemporary scholars refer to as the 'epistolary prescript', consisting of the identification of the author (the sender), the identification of the addressee(s), and a salutation. The author's name, often with honorific titles and the names of coauthors and information about them, are put in the nominative case. The addressees, sometimes along with their titles and information about them, are put in the dative case. Then a salutation, which can consist of the single word *chairein*, is added. In 2 Thess. 1.1-2, the epistolary prescript begins an *exordium*. It serves the important task of quite officially identifying the author as Paul, along with his co-senders Silvanus and Timothy. If this letter is Deuteropauline, the identity of this letter with Paul and his *ēthos* is central to its message, since our author then speaks in Paul's name and with his authority, and since Aristotle advised that the *ēthos* of the orator is one of the elements of persuasion.[2] The addressees are identified as 'the Church of the

Thessalonians in God our Father and [our] Lord Jesus Christ'. With
the possible exception of the second 'our' which does not appear in
the earliest and best manuscripts of 1 Thess. 1.1, this identification of
the addressees in 2 Thessalonians is identical with that in 1
Thessalonians. The full salutation of 2 Thess. 1.2 is the typical one in
the Pauline corpus.[3] The salutation, *charis hymin kai eirēnē* . . .
('grace to you and peace . . . ') may be a Pauline adaptation of the
conventional epistolary *chairein* into a specifically Christian greeting.[4]
Since this adaptation appears not to have been done by anybody
before Paul, if 2 Thessalonians is Deuteropauline, we have another
example of our author's writing with the literary *ēthos* of Paul.

The next part of the *exordium* is, form-critically, a prayer of
thanksgiving which depicts Paul as praying on behalf of the
Thessalonians and by extension, especially if this is a Deuteropauline
work, on behalf of any of its readers. As Cicero knew, prayers have
strong rhetorical value, and it is no accident that he discussed them
in his treatment of methods of acquiring goodwill in the *exordium*.[5]
The rhetor who makes an appeal to Heaven in effect gives his case
supernatural strength, since he is appealing to the highest judge and
court. The rhetorical power of prayers is enhanced by the specific
content of the prayers. Paul Schubert in his famous work, *Form and
Function of the Pauline Thanksgivings*, pointed out that the thanksgiving prayers in papyrus letters (to which he compared the letters
of the Pauline corpus) had particular and well-established functions
within the larger scheme of the letters. 'The function of the
epistolary thanksgiving in the papyrus letters is to focus the
epistolary situation, i.e., to introduce the vital theme of the letter.'[6]
This is to say that the issues raised in the thanksgiving prayers at the
beginnings of letters of this type tend to constitute the major
concerns of the letters. Ancient rhetorical theory explains very well
why this part of letters can function as a 'table of contents' of the
letter.[7] The reason is because of the genius of the literary form of the
thanksgiving prayer, namely the fact that in thanksgiving prayers the
author of the prayer has the literary opportunity to thank God, and
most especially to give specific reasons for doing so, reasons which
frequently do honor to the readers of the letter. Hence epistolary
thanksgiving prayers seem generally to function so as to acquire the
goodwill of the readers and to tell them the subjects of the letter,
which is the same general function as that of the *exordium* in
rhetoric. In the Pauline corpus, thanksgiving prayers of this sort are

usually related to the success of missionary activity. The writer of
2 Thessalonians portrays the apostle Paul as being thankful in 1.3-5
for the missionary success of the Thessalonians, namely the fact that
their faithfulness has increased and their love for each other has
multiplied. The fact of their increased faithfulness and love is what
Paul is able to boast about in his communications with other
churches. In verse 4, the key factor that is the major reason for
boasting is *hypomonē*, 'patience' or 'endurance'. The 'endurance' that
the Thessalonians have shown has been in the midst of (and in
response to) all of the trials and tribulations which they have
undergone. The author explains that the presence of the trials and
tribulations is 'evidence' (*endeigma*) of the righteous judgment of
God (1.5), trials which will make the Thessalonians 'worthy of the
kingdom of God, for which you are suffering'. Another reason for
thanksgiving is that, according to 1.6, it is 'right' for God to pay back
with tribulation those who are causing tribulation for the readers. An
additional reason for thanksgiving is that God will give rest, along
with 'us', to the oppressed at the revelation of Christ at Christ's
parousia. Other material in vv. 7-10 is related to the apocalyptic
theology being presented and is ultimately a cause for thanksgiving
by 'Paul' as well, since these apocalyptic events will separate the elect
from the damned, and God's justice will be done to the unrighteous
who are, to be sure, 'those who do not obey the Gospel' (1.8).

In the rhetorical summary at the end of this chapter, I have
analyzed the thanksgiving prayer around what seems to be its main
rhetorical function, that is, to tell the audience the reasons for which
the author is thankful to God. These reasons for thanksgiving
function so as to advise the audience of the rewards and punishments
that lie in store for the righteous and the unrighteous in the future, a
future controlled by God. The response that the readers of 2
Thessalonians make to this missive—responses presumably at both
the doctrinal and the practical levels (as seen in what is argued in ch.
2 and urged in ch. 3)—will serve to determine the readers' future
destiny.

There are six reasons for thanksgiving in the *exordium*. The first
three reasons in 1.3-4 are traditional parts of Pauline missionary
theology. The author portrays Paul here thanking God for the
missionary successes defined as the 'growth of faith' and 'increase of
love', and for the result of these successes, the fact that Paul may
rightly boast of the Thessalonians among the other churches. It is

significant to note that the first two of these three reasons are also found in 1 Thess. 1.3, 'faith' and 'love'. A fourth reason for Paul's thanksgiving found at 1 Thess. 1.3 is *hypomonē*, 'patience' or 'endurance'. If 2 Thessalonians is literarily dependent on 1 Thessalonians, one of the most striking transitions from 1 Thessalonians to 2 Thessalonians is the understanding of *hypomonē*. In 1 Thess. 1.3 it is spoken of as the 'patience of the hope of our Lord Jesus Christ', an apocalyptic idea, to be sure, in that the 'hope' is based on the expectation of the parousia of Christ, which in 1 Thessalonians appears to be quite eminent. However, in 2 Thess. 1.4ff. the content of *hypomonē* is enlarged so as to constitute the virtue of endurance during the unpleasant present apocalyptic consequences of being one of the elect. In fact, Paul's boasting (1.4) is precisely of the Thessalonians' *hypomonē* and *pistis* (here perhaps to be translated as 'faithfulness') in the face of the 'trials and tribulations' which they are undergoing. Thus, even the trials and tribulations which they are undergoing are a fifth reason for thanksgiving to God, since these sufferings are an 'evidence' of the righteous judgment of God (1.5). The sixth and final reason for thanksgiving is that these very sufferings are calculated precisely by God to make the elect 'worthy of the kingdom of God, for which you are suffering'.

In 1.6-10, the final three reasons for thanksgiving related to apocalyptic theology which were found in 1.4-5 are expanded upon and explained. In 1.6-7, endurance under trials is explained as a reason for thanksgiving because God will give negative and positive rewards to people based on their response to him: on those who afflict the readers God will work his revenge, but to the elect God will give rest. The fifth reason, the fact that the sufferings of the elect are evidence of the righteous judgment of God, is expanded upon in 1.7-10 by specifying the circumstances of the righteous judgment; this specification is constituted by a retelling of traditional apocalyptic material, complete with angels, fire, divine revenge, and the dazzling appearance of Christ.[8] Most important for the doctrine of 2 Thessalonians and the response to it that is urged is the explanation in 1.10 of the sixth reason for thanksgiving, namely that the sufferings would make the elect 'worthy of the kingdom of God'. The explanation is given in 1.10: the cause of the elect's being made worthy of the kingdom of God is 'because our [= Paul's] witness was believed by you on that day'.[9] This suggests that a negative corollary is also operative here, that those who do not believe the witness of Paul will not be found worthy of God's Kingdom. Therefore, the readers of this rhetorical discourse are being presented here with the two and only two sure outcomes of their possible responses to the discourse. One may either believe (or 'be faithful to') Paul's witness and be among the elect, or one may be among 'those who do not know God and do not obey the Gospel of our Lord Jesus' (1.8), and who will thus suffer 'eternal destruction away from the presence of the Lord and from the glory of his strength' (1.9). The presentation of crucial alternatives based on the course of action that the audience will take is consistent with the goals of rhetoric, especially deliberative rhetoric.[10] While forensic rhetoric is concerned with the defense (or prosecution) of someone on the basis of his or her past conduct, and epideictic rhetoric generally concerns itself with the praise or blame of persons or things in the present time (although according to Aristotle it can concern itself with the past and future as well[11]), deliberative rhetoric basically concerns itself with the advising of deliberative bodies as to proposed courses of action and their outcomes in the future.[12] Hence the rhetoric of 2 Thessalonians is consistent with the deliberative genus of rhetoric.

After the thanksgiving prayer is an intercessory prayer in 1.11-12. Just as Demosthenes did at the beginning of his *Epistle* 1, and just as the young Cicero advised, it appears that our author is here again attempting to gain the goodwill of his audience through a prayer.[13] Moreover, the basic petition of the prayer is that God will make the Thessalonians 'worthy of his calling' (1.11). This is to be accomplished in two related ways in 1.11-12. First, the 'making worthy' is to be accomplished through the manifestations of his will in 'every good purpose of holiness' and '[every] work of faith and power'. This is to say that the readers are urged to be 'made worthy' of God's calling through the living of their lives in holiness (as opposed to either false doctrine or immorality, or both) and appropriate 'works' of 'faith and power'. This seems to be an early reference to the commands to work in 2 Thessalonians 3. Both of these means imply the avoidance of acting *ataktōs* as in 3.1-15.

The *exordium* is ended with a flourish by our author in 1.12 by the mention of God. If God is to make the readers worthy of his calling, as our author prays in 1.11, through the two means of manifestation of his will, 'holiness' and 'works' of 'faith and power', the ultimate effect of this will be that the 'Name of our Lord Jesus will be glorified in you, according to the grace of our God and of [our] Lord Jesus Christ' (1.12). This is the desired religious effect of the intercessory prayer. Our author, however, appears at least as concerned with its rhetorical effect. He has already acted in the *exordium* to bring forward the *ēthos* of Paul. Thus 1.12 serves as a reminder to the readers that our author wishes to use not only Paul's *ēthos* to persuade but also the *ēthos* of Christ, whose doctrine he is teaching and whose name our author and his readers bear as Christians. Thus the readers of this document are advised to follow its doctrine for yet another reason, namely the 'glorification' of the name of Christ. The negative corollary may also be assumed: if the readers do not choose to follow the doctrine of this epistle, they will be dishonoring the name of Christ, with its attendant consequences.

2.1-2, the partitio. The *partitio* can function in two ways, either as a listing of the problems to be dealt with in the proof or as a statement of agreement and disagreement with adversaries.[14] In Cicero's *De inventione* 1.31-33, the *partitio* may take either of two forms, either a statement of agreement and disagreement with one's adversary, or a statement of matters to be argued in the proof. In the *Institutio oratoria* 4.5.1ff., Quintilian understands the *partitio* to be a section where propositions are enumerated, both those of one's own and of one's adversary.

The *partitio* in 2 Thessalonians seems to be more like that described by Quintilian than that described by Cicero. Specifically, in 2.1-2 the author has briefly alluded to the points to be argued, which in fact includes the great point of disagreement with his adversaries, namely 'that the Day of the Lord has already come' (2.2). This doctrinal point is also alluded to in 2.1, in that two eschatological events are mentioned there, namely the 'parousia of our Lord Jesus Christ' and 'our being gathered up with him'.[15] What is being referred to in the point of disagreement and by these two eschatological events is the subject of the first proof, which is a *refutatio* of a heretical eschatology, by means of our author's 'orthodox' eschatology. What is being refuted is precisely the doctrine stated in 2.2, 'that the Day of the Lord has already come'. Also in 2.2 is the identification of the possible sources of the heretical doctrine, sources which are listed: 'whether by spirit, or by *logos* or by an epistle as from us. . . '[16] This identification of sources of the heretical doctrine is of great interest, especially since 'spirit' and

Paul's (presumably originally oral) teaching are sources of authority quite well known to readers of other letters in the Pauline corpus. And, notably, our author's sources of correct doctrine as listed in 2.15 include *logos* and 'epistle', but *not* 'spirit'. Thus our author implies that 'spirit' (or 'the Spirit') may *not* be a source of appropriate doctrine for his readers. This is an extremely significant part of the theology of 2 Thessalonians, a theology different from the theology (or theologies) of the undisputed Pauline letters. The suggestion that the Spirit is a source of false doctrine in 2 Thess. 2.15 makes a particularly jarring contrast with 1 Thess. 5.19f. where Paul's readers are exhorted, 'Do not quench the Spirit' and 'Do not despise prophecy'.

Also alluded to in 2 Thess. 2.2 is the notion of stability. The readers are urged not to let the heretical eschatology cause them to be 'quickly shaken up from your state of mind nor disturbed'. I read this as an allusion to the second proof in 2.13-15, in which our author assures his readers that they are not heretical believers since they are 'brethren beloved by the Lord' (2.13) and they have been 'chosen' and 'called' by God (2.13-14), 'through our [= Paul's] gospel so as to obtain the glory of our Lord Jesus Christ'. Though the 'spirit' (or 'Spirit') is mentioned in 2.13, its activity is spoken of as 'sanctification' rather than empowerment through spiritual gifts as in Corinthians, Galatians, and Romans. Indeed, the goal of the second proof appears to be the readers' personal and doctrinal stability, as the readers are urged to 'stand up and be strong in the traditions which you were taught' (2.15), which is exactly the opposite of succumbing to those who would 'shake you up' and 'disturb you' (2.2) with their heretical doctrine.

2.3-15, the probatio. Like the proof of Demosthenes' *Epistle* 1, this proof is in two parts, 2.3-12 and 2.13-15. The first part of the proof is specifically a refutation of the heretical eschatology mentioned in 2.2, the teaching done by our author's theological enemies 'that the Day of the Lord has already come'. This heretical eschatology is refuted by means of an alternate eschatology stated as an eschatological 'timetable'. The goal of this timetable is to show that the Day of the Lord cannot have come yet, since the prerequisite cosmic events have not yet happened. Hence the timetable and its exposition are themselves the first proof, since they are precisely the means by which the *refutatio* of the heretical doctrine, 'that the Day of the Lord has already come', is being argued.

2 Thess. 2.3a begins a new section with a warning. The warning against deception is a traditional part of apocalyptic, and it is consistent with the delusion which God will send in 2.11 on those who are destined to believe the heretical theology and thus to be damned. The warning against deception is traditional; we see traces of it in 1 Cor. 6.9 and 15.33 in connection with false doctrine, both with the phrase 'Don't be fooled!'[17] Actually, the warning against deception is itself apocalyptic, because it threatens the reader with an undesirable eschatological fate if the warning is not properly heeded.

2 Thess. 2.3b-4 sets before the reader the beginning of a timetable of apocalyptic events. The timetable looks schematically like this:

1. 'now': Restraint\
2. 'first': Rebellion
3. 'then': Revelation of the Man of Lawlessness
4. (immediately upon #3): Appearance of Jesus to destroy the Man of Lawlessness.

The thesis, that the Day of the Lord has *not* already come, is to be demonstrated by the setting forth of conditions in the form of apocalyptic signs necessary for the Day of the Lord to come. Before the Day of the Lord can come, there must be a rebellion, *apostasia*, and then the revelation of the Man of Lawlessness. What is this rebellion? Walter Bauer's lexicon defines *apostasia* as 'rebellion', and shows that it has both political and religious senses from the secular occurrences of it in Greek literature.[18] Béda Rigaux builds on this and shows that it is used in the religious sense in the Septuagint, namely at Josh. 22.22 ; Jer. 2.19; 2 Chron. 28.19; 33.19; 1 Maccabees 2.15; and very notably in the apocryphal *Ascension of Isaiah* 2.4.[19] In the *Ascension of Isaiah*, *apostasia* seems to be defined in a combination of senses including a religious sense, in 2.5 of that document also including witchcraft, magic, fornication, adultery, etc. However, in 2 Thessalonians the exact meaning of *apostasia* is not defined. None of the commentators suggests that vv. 3b-4 function as part of a rhetorical proof, and thus most of the commentators condemn themselves to the futile task of trying to find the exact parallels and meanings of these words. From a rhetorical point of view, however, it would seem that the identification of loaded words like *apostasia* do not need to be exact; in fact, it would be to the advantage of our author to make the semantic horizons of his words as broad as possible, in order to make it clear that the apocalyptic signs have not happened, and thus that the Day of the Lord has not already come.

Obviously the Man of Lawlessness, who is also referred to in 2 Thessalonians as the 'Son of Perdition', is a quasi-divine figure, a kind of evil 'divine man', some intermediate figure between God and humanity. In Greek tradition, this figure could easily be identified with a *daimôn* or some other intermediary figure.[20] In Hebrew tradition, this figure would likely be Satan, who characteristically is the chief opponent to God. However, in 2 Thess. 2.4, there seems to be an allusion to the historical tradition of Antiochus IV Epiphanes who desecrated the Jerusalem Temple by the institution of the worship of Zeus Olympus in the Temple. He also issued money that depicted himself and included a superscription referring to himself as *theos*.[21] From a rhetorical point of view it is not necessary to decide which, if any single, tradition is being alluded to, since the rhetorical force of 2.3-12 is to show that the Day of the Lord cannot have happened yet, because the unmistakable cosmic signs have not happened. In fact, to point out that it is a ruler of cosmic significance who is being discussed, our author adds that the activity of the Man of Lawlessness is empowered by Satan in 2.9.

The eschatological timetable itself in vv. 3b-4 is interesting. There are other such timetables in the New Testament, especially in Mt. 24.3-8, where the signs before the end are revealed to the reader. There are extensive parallels in the book of Revelation. One aspect of such material is that there exists a cosmic plan whereby the state of the world must get more and more evil before the eschatological judge/savior is to come.[22] 2 Thessalonians has a strongly pessimistic outlook on the world, an outlook which is often, though not always, found in apocalyptic literature.[23]

2 Thess. 2.5 sets before the reader the identification of 2 Thessalonians' teaching with Paul's oral teaching, as opposed to the teaching of the false doctrine in 2.2. The identification with Pauline teaching also fits the exhortation in 2.15 to 'stand firm and hold fast to the traditions which you were taught, whether by *logos* or epistle'.

Traditionally, the most difficult part of the letter to translate and to understand is 2.6-7. These verses refer cryptically to some restraining factor which, even more cryptically, 'Paul' says that the Thessalonians already know. There has been no lack of imagination on the part of New Testament scholars in identifying what *to katechon* ('the Restrainer', neuter) is and who *ho katechōn* ('the Restrainer', masculine) is. These answers have included the Roman state and the Roman emperor, as well as the phenomenon of the binding of Satan or evil by an angel of God. Oscar Cullmann has suggested that the restraining factor is the missionary activity of Paul and the restrainer Paul himself, a suggestion that goes back as far as Theodore of Mopsuestia.[24] More recently Charles H. Giblin in his lengthy monograph devoted to 2 Thessalonians 2 has suggested that the restraining factor should be translated as the 'seizing force' and the restrainer should be translated as the 'Seizer', who seems to be an unknown individual using this force. Joseph Coppens of Louvain suggested that what are meant are the 'mystery of lawlessness' and the 'Man of Lawlessness', although it is scarcely explainable how the mystery of lawlessness can be the restraining factor on the Man of Lawlessness. Wolfgang Trilling has suggested that the *katechon* is the function of delaying and that it is from God. Roger D. Aus suggests that, since there are several word parallels to Isaiah 66 (Septuagint) scattered throughout the chapter, and since Isaiah 66.6 does talk about God's restraining, the restrainer in 2 Thessalonians 2 is God.[25] It seems logical (insofar as apocalyptic is logical) that God should be the one to restrain someone who is given supernatural power by the Evil One. The activity of restraining in 2.6-7 is perhaps also explained by 2.11-12 where it is clear that God is behind the scenes as the planner and executor of apocalyptic events.

The timetable continues in 2.8-12. 'And then' indicates the next event in the apocalyptic timetable, i.e. the revelation of the Man of Lawlessness, here referred to as the Lawless One. At v. 8 there seems to be a clear parallel to Isa. 11.4b (Septuagint): 'And he shall smite the earth with a word from his mouth, and with the breath between his lips he shall kill the irreligious'.[26] Elsewhere in the New Testament, fairly clear parallels are found in Rev. 19.15, 20; cf. 1 Tim. 6.14; 2 Tim. 1.10; 4.1, 8; Tit. 2.13; all of which refer to the coming of Christ at the Day of Judgment. The epiphany of the Lawless One is described in terms similar to those of Christ's epiphany, most notably with the phrase that had become formulaic, 'signs and wonders'.[27]

In Rev. 13.13, the evil man will deceive many people through his 'signs and wonders'; however, in 2 Thess. 2.11 it is God who sends a delusion on the opponents of 2 Thessalonians—the heretics whose religious faith is perverse and dangerous. The delusion of believers is a standard apocalyptic topic.[28] But here the topic of divine delusion is used in a special way. Here God sends the delusion, but there is a special identification of the deluded people: they are, in fact, the ones who refused to believe the orthodox doctrine and thus took pleasure in heresy, here characterized as 'the lie' and 'unrighteousness' in 2.11.

I have analyzed 2.13-15 as the second part of the proof. It presupposes and builds on the first part of the proof in that the heretical doctrine has been identified and in that there is now no doubt that the heretical doctrine is false and dangerous. In this second proof, our author seems to pick up the 'friendship' topics which are so frequent in 1 Thessalonians.[29] But in 2 Thessalonians these topics are used in a different way, namely, to reinforce the orthodox believers in their correct theology.

Since the second part of the proof seems to pick up on the topics of friendship, I have analyzed it in three parts, based on the three crucial relationships involved: (1) Paul's relationship with the readers; (2) God's relationship with the readers; and (3) the readers' relationship with Paul, who is here understood as the source of correct doctrine. All three of these relationships demonstrate that the readers will be on the favorable side of things at the Day of the Lord, but only if the readers stand firm in these relationships.

The notion of God's election of believers picks up on older missionary language which we see scattered in the New Testament, notably the motif of God's choosing the believers as 'firstfruits', a term borrowed from an agricultural-cultic context, but which evidently indicates an early missionary success.[30] Another part of God's activity is also listed separately from the topic of election, namely, that of 'vocation'. This term, too, recalls other missionary language seen elsewhere in the New Testament.[31] These two notions of election and vocation presuppose a theory of how Christian missionary activity works. First, God does the choosing and calling, and then human workers go into the field and evangelize. A somewhat different view of mission is seen in 1 Cor. 3.6ff. where Paul planted, Apollos watered, but God gave growth, although in either case, God's activity is the *sine qua non* of mission.

2.16-17, the peroratio. Like quite a few other *perorationes*, the one in 2 Thessalonians involves a prayer.[32] Since the two-part proof in 2.3-15 seems primarily directed towards the doctrinal orthodoxy of the readers and their personal and doctrinal stability, it is not at all surprising that the *peroratio* which sums up this two-part proof should be an intercessory prayer for the readers, specifically asking the deity to do to or for the readers what the proofs have already sought to persuade them to do. Thus the deity is brought in as a part of our author's rhetoric.[33] Also, certain important goals of the *exordium* are shared with those of the *peroratio*. Obviously it is always to the rhetor's advantage for his audience to be *benevolens, attentus, et docilis* ('well disposed, attentive, and ready to receive instruction') no matter how far along in the discourse the rhetor is. Hence Aristotle's exposition of the *peroratio* begins with the task of disposing the audience favorably towards the rhetor, along with disposing them unfavorably towards the adversary, as well as amplification and deprecation, excitement of the emotion of the audience, and recapitulation.[34] What better way could be found to make the readers of 2 Thessalonians well disposed to our author's message than to have Paul, the founding apostle of many churches, intercede with God for them? And more especially, since our author is evidently so interested in his readers' doctrinal orthodoxy (namely, that they agree with the theology of this letter), and their stability in emotional and spiritual outlook, what better way to bring this about than to ask God to give it to them? And if the readers of this letter fail to understand the doctrine in 2.3-12, and in fact get 'shaken up' by the false doctrine, what more significant activity could there be than to assure the readers that they will receive their eschatological reward, when the Day of the Lord does finally come? In fact, the theology of 2 Thessalonians includes the aretalogy of God the Father in the prayer in 2.16. God is described here as a deity who 'loves', 'comforts', and 'gives hope' to 'us'. Also, the petition of the prayer in 2.17 serves to remind the readers of the proofs. The second part of the proof is alluded to by the petition asking God to 'comfort' the readers' 'hearts'. The first part of the proof, much more strictly doctrinal, is referred to by the petition to establish the readers' hearts in 'every good *logos*', namely, every correct kind of teaching. Finally, the content of what is to follow in ch. 3 is alluded to by the petition to establish the readers' hearts in 'every good work'.

The phraseology of the prayer in 2.16-17 is interesting in itself. Whereas the prayer in the clear 1 Thessalonians parallel had mentioned God first and then Jesus, the prayer in 2 Thessalonians reverses this order, but then includes an aretalogy which evidently relates to the Father. The activities of the Father are especially striking, in the context of this epistle. 'Love' we would expect, but the giving of 'eternal consolation' could be borrowed from Rom. 16.5 or 2 Cor. 1.7. It is unclear whether our author here is borrowing from other Pauline letters when he needs some resonant phrases to amplify the section (one of the traditional goals of the *peroratio*), but it is possible that this baroque phrase has been preserved in the Pauline churches through continued liturgical use.

3.1-15, the exhortation. The exhortation is not a traditional *pars orationis* from the Graeco-Roman rhetorical handbook tradition. A number of suggestions have been made as to its origin. Betz sees close parallels to the exhortation (which he calls the *exhortatio*) in paraenetic material at the ends of philosophical letters, although the connection between such letters and Pauline letters is not made clear by him.[35] The major problem, however, with Betz's treatment of the rhetoric of Galatians is his identification of Galatians as an example of forensic rhetoric. Although Galatians certainly does have important features of forensic rhetoric, especially Paul's defense of himself, based on things which have happened in the past, George A. Kennedy points out that, 'It seems unlikely that anyone reading through Galatians at one sitting would conclude that it is an apology rather than an attempt to persuade the Galatians, swayed by other advisers, what they should do'. Hence Kennedy correctly identifies the major rhetorical *genus* of Galatians as deliberative rhetoric, and thus he is better able to account for the presence of exhortation in Gal. 5.1–6.10 on the basis of that *genus*, which consists of two parts, exhortation and dissuasion.[36] As chapter two of this study showed, Demosthenes's *Epistle* 1 contained a section of exhortation near the end of the letter. Also, so-called 'nonliterary' Greek letters which were written on papyri provide plausible parallels to the 'exhortation' sections of Pauline letters. In Greek epistolography (particularly in the Hellenistic period), letters often include requests before the final greetings. Such requests may be large or small, single or multiple, but they frequently form an important part of the letter, in fact sometimes the major reason why the letter was written. Hence, even though exhortation is not a standard *pars orationis*, we are justified in identifying certain sections of certain letters in the Pauline corpus as exhortation sections, because of a variety of parallels to both 'literary' and 'nonliterary' letters,[37] and because of the strong connection of deliberative rhetoric to exhortation.[38]

The exhortation in 2 Thessalonians is in 3.1-15. It seems to have three parts, a command (or perhaps a request) to pray for Paul in 3.1-4, an intercessory prayer for the readers in 3.5, and a very elaborate section in 3.6-15 in which a command to work is stated in four different ways.

In 3.1-4, readers are asked to pray for Paul with especial attention to the mission of the Pauline churches. Positively, the petition of the prayer in 3.1 is that the 'Word of the Lord' may triumph. The negative corollary of this is stated in 3.2, namely that Paul may be delivered from 'untoward and wicked people'. These persons are compared with God in 3.2-3: 'for not all [human beings] are faithful'—namely the wicked people—but 'God is faithful'. This rhetorically implies to the readers that they should be faithful, imitating God rather than the 'untoward and wicked people'. Hence if the readers' *imitatio* is of the right sort, then God will 'strengthen' and 'guard' them from evil (3.3). 3.4 expresses the hope, by stating it as a fact, that the teachings of this epistle will be followed: 'we are convinced ... that you are doing and you will do'. The extension from present obedience to future obedience bespeaks the *genus* of deliberative rhetoric, whose focus is the alteration of policy and behavior in the future.

A further intercessory prayer is in 3.5, whose petition is that 'the Lord' may direct the hearts of the readers 'to the love of God and the *hypomonē* of Christ'. In the larger context of 2 Thessalonians, both love and endurance are needed by the readers, since a sign of the elect is suffering, through which one may become 'worthy of the Kingdom of God' (1.5), and since even apostles are afflicted by 'untoward and evil people', of whom it is rightly said, 'not all are faithful' (3.2). The correct response to this prayer in 3.5 is the *imitatio Dei* by the readers, so that they may possess and exhibit both love and patience. The opposite of the prayer is also implicit: the 'untoward and wicked people' (3.2) are precisely those whose 'hearts' are *not* directed 'to the love of God and the patience of Christ'.

3.6-15 contains the paraenesis of the letter. The paraenesis is summed up in a single command to work which is stated in four different ways. First in 3.6, the command is stated negatively: 'We beseech you, brothers, in the Name of [our] Lord Jesus Christ to keep away from every idle brother who is acting *ataktōs* ['out of line'] and not according to the tradition which has been handed on by us'. The adverb *ataktōs* recalls 1 Thess. 5.14, where Paul gives the command to 'admonish the *ataktoi*', al though Paul clearly leaves the identity of the *ataktoi* open, since he does not reveal who the *ataktoi* are or what *taxis* they are violating. It appears that 2 Thessalonians picks up on Paul's openendedness and expands upon it, giving the *ataktoi* several identifications. In 2 Thessalonians 3, the *ataktoi* are evidently lazy Christians who 'sponge' off the rest of the community. This seems to be at the practical level; 2 Thessalonians does not tell us that they are the same people who are so broadly condemned on ch. 1 and 2 of this epistle because of heresy. The 'tradition handed on by us' in 3.6 is evidently defined in 3.7-9, where the readers are exhorted to imitate Paul, namely his habit of not eating anyone's bread without paying for it, although in 3.9 there is the disclaimer by our author that Paul had the right to support by the Church, but he preferred to give a good example to the flock. The example is recounted in 3.8, where our author says that Paul 'worked with toil and labor, by night and day'. The command to work is stated again in 3.10-11, where the command to work is identified not only with Paul's example (as in 3.8), but with Paul's oral teaching when he was with the Thessalonians: 'And indeed when we were with you, we advised you this very thing, that if someone did not wish to work, let him not eat'. Nevertheless, our author is forced to admit in 3.11 that this command was not obeyed: 'For we have heard of some among you acting *ataktōs*, not working but being busybodies'. Since the command to work had historically not been successful, according to our author, during Paul's residence with the church in Thessalonika, it is restated by our author in the present in 3.12-15. Our author's authority to give this command is prominently mentioned in 3.12, 'our Lord Jesus Christ', as well as his specification that the disobeyers of the old command must obey this new command. The new command is that the readers must 'work with quietness' to 'eat their own bread', that is, to earn their own living. A negative corollary is stated in 3.13, that the readers (as they wait for the Day of the Lord which will be a long time in coming, according to ch. 2) should not get weary in doing good works. Nevertheless, our author must realize that this epistolary command is as unlikely to be obeyed as was Paul's oral command, so he gives in 3.14 rules for enforcement of the command: 'If anyone does not obey our *logos* through [this] epistle, point him out, so as not to associate with him, that he may be ashamed'. Yet in 3.15 it is recognized that there are limits to ostracism: 'And do not consider him as an enemy, but counsel him as a brother'. In other words, the model of family must prevail within the Christian community, even though certain members of the family act like 'black sheep' and must be punished to maintain family stability, as Dennis E. Groh has recently pointed out.[39] The alternative to rules and guidelines such as in 2 Thess. 3.14-15 would be a community which had no limits and thus no definition, something with which the author of 2 Thessalonians would not be pleased.

3.16-18, the epistolary postscript. The epistolary postscript is not a traditional part of a rhetorical discourse, but it is a traditional part of Greek letters; hence it is analyzed under a separate heading in this study.

The intercessory prayer is a prayer for peace for the readers, 'always, in every way'. It is especially appropriate just after the command to work and to ostracize anybody who does not work in 3.14-15, even with the general guideline that fellow Christians must be treated as brothers, not enemies. The prayer for peace is also appropriate to the whole letter, given the apocalyptic doctrine of chs. 1 and 2, and perhaps also given the doctrines of our author's theological enemies which are 'shaking up' the readers (2.2). The prayer for peace is appropriately addressed to 'the Lord of peace himself', another example of how the theology of the prayer is partially expressed by the attributes of the deity to whom the prayer is addressed.

The authentication in 3.17 is of great interest, since it attempts to authenticate *this* letter, as opposed to 'a letter as from us [= Paul]' which is a source of heresy, according to 2.2. This evidently points to the fact that conflict within Pauline Christianity is being fought upon the battleground of letters. It does seem unlikely that the authentic Paul, who seems to use rhetoric very well in his genuine letters, would even remotely suggest that 'a letter from us' should be held in doubt, since they are the closest thing to Paul's physical presence that most of his churches have at any given time.[40] Rather, the genuine Paul seems quite well aware that his letters are indeed 'weighty and strong', as his enemies are forced to admit (2 Cor. 10.10). The last thing that any competent rhetor would wish to do would be to deprecate the forcefulness of his rhetoric, either his public oratory or his literary rhetoric. Thus, the scenario which the defenders of Pauline authorship are forced to draw, in which the authentic Paul, who had recently written 1 Thessalonians to an early congregation of his, now writes 2 Thessalonians in order to warn them against 'letters as from us' which have a heretical theology, is from a rhetorical point of view extremely implausible.[41] An alternative scenario which I work out in Chapter 4 of this study is a situation in the Pauline churches after the death of Paul, which is the only time we really know pseudonymous Pauline letters to have existed. In this post pauline period, it is evident that many forces in the churches wished to authenticate themselves with the *ēthos* of Paul, both 'heretical' and 'orthodox', if it is right to use these terms.[42] Given the variety of forces after Paul's death, the attempt at authentication in 3.17 is quite understandable: 'The greeting is in my—Paul's—hand, and it is the sign in every epistle of how I write'. No convincing *Sitz im Leben* has ever been deduced for the words 'in every epistle', if these words must be understood to come from Paul himself, particularly if 1 and 2 Thessalonians are dated relatively early during the writing career of Paul, especially if 1 Thessalonians is the only previous letter which the Thessalonians have received from Paul, and since no authenticating 'sign' appears at the end of that epistle. The clear implication of the 'sign' is that letters without this signature and 'sign' are forgeries.

The final prayer in 3.18 ends the letter with a prayer for the 'grace of our Lord Jesus Christ' to be 'with all of you', a prayer which could be borrowed from Rom. 16.24, but which has much similarity to the typical Pauline epistolary salutation, 'Grace to you and peace . . .' Hence the epistolary postscript, like the epistolary prescript, tends to project the *ēthos* of Paul in an important way into this letter, making this letter as persuasive as our author knows how.

For the purpose of seeing the rhetorical structure of this letter as a whole, I add a rhetorical summary of 2 Thessalonians and its *partes* in outline form.

A Rhetorical Summary of 2 Thessalonians

1.1-12	I.	Exordium
1.1-2	A.	Epistolary Prescript
1.1		1. Sender: Paul
		2. Co-senders: Silvanus & Timothy
		3. Addressees: 'The Church of the Thessalonians. . .'
1.2		4. Salutation
1.3-10	B.	Thanksgiving Prayer
1.3		1. Orant: 'we'
		2. Mode of Prayer: 'we are obliged'
		3. Deity invoked: God
		4. Time of prayer: always
		5. Persons prayed for: Thessalonians. Address: 'brothers'
1.3-10		6. Reasons for thanksgiving
1.3		a. Three reasons related to missionary success
		i. Definition of missionary success: growth of faith
		ii. Definition of missionary success: increase of love
1.4		iii. Result of missionary success: Paul's boasting
		b. Three reasons related to apocalyptic theology
		i. Endurance under persecution
1.5		ii. Description of endurance: evidence of the righteous judgment of God
		iii. Result of endurance: being found worthy of the Kingdom of God
1.6-10		c. Explanations of reasons related to apocalyptic
1.6		theology
		i. Reasons for endurance
		(a) Negatively: Divine revenge on those who afflict readers
1.7		(b) Positively: Rest to the oppressed
1.7-9		ii. Specification of circumstances of God's righteous judgment
		(a) Time
1.7		(b) Place
		(c) Personnel: 'angels of his power'
1.8		(d) Equipment: 'with a flame of fire'
1.8		(e) Results: revenge
		(1) Specification of recipients:
		(A) Negatively
		(B) Negatively
1.9		(2) Specification of content of revenge

1.10			iii. Reason for being found worthy of the Kingdom: Paul's witness was believed
1.11-12	C.		Intercessory Prayer
1.11		1.	Reason for prayer: 'for this reason' (referring to foregoing material)
		2.	Orant: 'we'
		3.	Time of prayer: always
		4.	Persons prayed for: readers
		5.	Deity invoked: God
1.11-12		6.	Petitions
			a. God to make readers worthy of his calling
			b. God to fulfill his will Manifestations of will:
			i. 'every good purpose of holiness'
			ii. '(every) work of faith and power'
1.12			c. Glorification of the Name of the Lord Jesus
			i. Positively: glorification of Name in readers
			ii. Conversely: glorification of readers in the Name
			iii. Means of glorification of Name: grace
2.1-2	II.	Partitio	
2.1-2	A.		Subjects to be dealt with in the probatio
2.1		1.	Eschatological events (first proof)
			a. Parousia of Christ
			b. Gathering of believers with Christ at Parousia
2.2		2.	Stability of readers (stated negatively): 'that you not be shaken up. . . ' (second proof)
2.2	B.		Point of disagreement (heresy to be refuted)
		1.	Identification of sources of heresy
			a. 'spirit [as from us]'
			b. '*logos* [as from us]'
			c. 'a letter as from us'
2.2		2.	Content of heresy: 'that the Day of the Lord has already come'
2.3-15	III.	Probatio	
2.3-12	A.		First proof (*refutatio*)
2.3a		1.	Warning against deception
			a. Statement of warning
			b. Means of deception
2.3b-10		2.	First argument: an apocalyptic timetable, according to which the Day of the Lord cannot have come yet
2.3b			a. First sign: rebellion Time of sign: 'first'
2.3b-4			b. Second sign: revelation of Man of Lawlessness
2.3b			i. Statement of sign
2.3b-4			ii. Aretalogy of Man of Lawlessness

<table>
<tr><td>2.3b</td><td></td><td></td><td>(a)</td><td>Alternative title: Son of Perdition</td></tr>
<tr><td>2.4</td><td></td><td></td><td>(b)</td><td>Activities</td></tr>
</table>

2.3b   (a) Alternative title: Son of Perdition
2.4   (b) Activities
        (1) Opposition to God
        (2) Exaltation of self
        (3) Seating of self in Temple
        (4) Proclamation of self as God
2.5   c. Identification of timetable as true Pauline doctrine
       i. Address: 'do you not remember?'
       ii. Identification of timetable with Paul's oral teaching
2.6-7   d. Happenings before the apocalyptic signs: explanation why they have not yet taken place
2.6   i. Time of restraining factor: 'now'
       ii. Address: 'you know'
       iii. Restraining factor: *katechon* (neuter)
       iv. Purpose of restraining factor: to reveal Man of Lawlessness 'in his own time'
2.7   v. Identity of activities of lawlessness
2.7a   (a) Time
        (b) Activity
        (c) Restraining factor: *katechōn* (masculine)
2.7b   (d) Duration of restraint: until Man of Lawlessness appears in midst
2.8   e. Third apocalyptic sign: destruction of Man of Lawlessness by Jesus
       i. Time: 'then'
       ii. Activity at which Jesus will intervene: revelation of Man of Lawlessness
       iii. Statement of third sign: Lord Jesus will kill
       iv. Means
        (a) Breath of Jesus' mouth
        (b) Lord Jesus' appearing and coming
2.9   f. Description of second sign: Parousia of Man of Lawlessness
       i. Means: Activity of Satan
2.10   ii. Results: Wicked deception
       iii. Doctrinal note: reason for perishing was refusal to love the truth
2.11   3. Explanation of God's activity behind the scenes at the signs
      a. Statement of activity: God sends delusion on heretics
      b. Results of delusion

2.11		i. Delusion compels heretics to believe heresy
2.12		ii. Condemnation of heretics
		iii. Doctrinal note: definition of heretics
2.12		(a) Negatively: did not believe truth
		(b) Positively: took pleasure in unrighteousness
2.13-15	B.	Second proof
2.13		1. First argument: Paul's relationship to the readers
		a. Reasons: Paul always bound to give thanks (cf. 1.3)
		b. Address: 'brethren beloved by the Lord'
2.13-14		2. Second argument: God's relationship to the readers Reasons:
2.13		a. God's election of readers
		i. Time of election
		ii. Destiny: salvation
		iii. Means
		(1) Sanctification in the Spirit
		(2) Readers' belief in the truth
2.14		b. God's vocation of readers
		i. Destiny
		ii. Means: Paul's gospel
		iii. Result: glory
2.15		3. Third argument: readers' orthodoxy will prove they are not heretics
		Responses to God's and Paul's activity urged:
		a. Stand firm
		b. Hold to traditions already taught
		i. Teacher: Paul
		ii. Modes of teaching
		(1) '[our] *logos*'
		(2) 'our epistle'
2.16-17 IV.		Peroratio (stated as an intercessory prayer)
2.16	A.	Orant: Paul
	B.	Persons prayed for: readers
	C.	Deities invoked
		1. Lord Jesus Christ
		2. God our Father
	D.	Aretalogy
		1. Identification of deity: Father
		2. Activities of deity:
		a. Love
		b. Comfort
		c. Giving of hope
		3. Recipients of divine activities: 'us'
		4. Means of divine activities: 'grace'

2.17	E.	Petitions

E. Petitions (2.17)
1. Comfort hearts of readers
2. Establish readers' hearts

V. Exhortation (3.1-15)

A. (3.1-4) Command (or request) to pray for Paul
1. Petitions to be prayed (for missionary success)
   - a. (3.1) Positively: Word of Lord to triumph
   - b. (3.2-3) Negatively: Paul's deliverance from untoward and wicked people
     - i. (3.2) Statement of petition
     - ii. Definition of wicked: 'not all are faithful'
     - iii. (3.3) Doctrinal note, *e contrario*: 'God is faithful'
   - c. (3.3) Result of prayer for Paul: God will strengthen and guard readers from evil
2. (3.4) Digression on obedience to command
   - a. Statement of confidence in readers
   - b. Reasons for confidence: Readers' obedience
     - i. Present
     - ii. Future

B. (3.5) Intercessory Prayer
1. (3.5) Orant: Paul
2. Persons prayed for: readers
3. Mode of prayer: performative
4. Deity invoked: 'the Lord'
5. Petition: direction of hearts of readers to love of God and *hypomonē* of Christ

C. (3.6-15) Command to work
1. (3.6) Paul's authority to command: Name of our Lord Jesus Christ
2. Command to work
   - a. Stated negatively: keep away from any idle brother
     - i. Statement of command
     - ii. (3.7-9) Definition of living 'in idleness': not according to tradition
   - b. Stated positively: imitate Paul
     - i. (3.7) Address: 'you know'
     - ii. Statement of command
     - iii. Definition of Paul's behavior to imitate
       - (1) Negatively: non-idleness
       - (2) (3.8) Negatively: not eating anyone's bread without paying
     - iv. (3.9) Result of Paul's good behavior: Paul not a burden
     - v. Disclaimer: Paul had the right to church support, but preferred to give example

3.10-11   c. Stated historically
3.10   i. Historical identification of command with Paul's oral teaching
      ii. Statement of command: 'if anyone will not work, let that person not eat'
3.11   iii. Unintended result of command: disobedience
3.12-13   d. Stated in the present
3.12   i. Authority: Lord Jesus Christ (cf. 3.6)
      ii. Recipients of new command: disobeyers of old command
3.12-13   iii. Statement of new command
3.12   (1) Positively: do work in quietness
      (2) Positively: earn own living
3.13   (3) Negatively: command against weariness in good works
3.14-15   3. Rules for enforcement of command to work
      a. Definition of violator: one who refuses to obey this letter
      b. Specification of punishment
      c. Intended result of punishment: violator to be ashamed
3.15   d. General guideline for punishment by ostracism: treat not as an enemy but as a brother
3.16-17 VI. Epistolary Postscript
3.16   A. Intercessory Prayer
      1. Orant: Paul
      2. Deity invoked: 'the Lord of peace'
      3. Persons prayed for: readers
      4. Petition: peace in all times in all ways
      5. Blessing: 'The Lord be with you'
3.17   B. Authentication
      1. Of this letter
      2. Of other letters with same signature
3.18   C. Final Blessing: 'The grace of Christ be with you'.

Conclusion

This chapter has proceeded by showing that 2 Thessalonians does correspond well with several traditional rhetorical precepts, including *partes orationis* and topics one often finds in deliberative discourses. The *partes* were indeed found in Demosthenes' *Epistle* 1, as analyzed in the previous chapter of this study. Every indication is that 2 Thessalonians is an intentionally worked-out document of deliberative rhetoric, with a clear goal: to refute those who say, 'whether by spirit or *logos* or a letter as from us, that the Day of the Lord has already come'. Additionally, the author has as a goal the correction of certain behavior in one or more early Christian communities, the behavior of people who evidently do not work for their living, and whose lack of working upsets (at least) our author. As advised in 1 Thessalonians, these *ataktoi* are to be admonished so that their behavior will come in line with a standard pleasing to our author. If these people's behavior will not conform, the erring persons are to be made ashamed by ostracism, yet still they are to be treated as Christians, which is paradoxical to say the least.

If this rhetorical analysis of 2 Thessalonians as an intentional document of deliberative rhetoric is basically correct, this means that earlier studies on 2 Thessalonians that do not use rhetorical precepts to guide the analyses made may be substantially revised. Additionally, if this study of 2 Thessalonians is essentially correct, then a further step must be taken: to attempt to 'get behind' the rhetoric to discern the motives of the author in writing this remarkable piece of theological polemic. What is 'behind' the rhetoric is an audience situation, that is, what is happening to one or more communities that provoked either an early Christian writer to write in Paul's name and thus with his *ēthos*. Thus, further study should explore what can be known about the history of Pauline Christianity in an attempt to piece together the conflict that clearly took place between our author and those who say, 'whether by spirit or *logos* or a letter from us, that the Day of the Lord has already come'. If such a conflict can be found, it is likely that 2 Thessalonians, a long-ignored and much misunderstood epistle, can give us a key to unlock a difficult segment of the history of Pauline Christianity. The remaining chapters of this study will attempt to locate 2 Thessalonians within the history of Pauline Christianity.

Chapter 4

2 THESSALONIANS AS A DEUTEROPAULINE LETTER

The Hypothesis of Pauline Authorship

In Chapter 1 of this study, the history of scholarship on 2 Thessalonians was briefly reviewed,[1] demonstrating several positions that scholars in recent centuries have taken concerning the authorship and purpose of 2 Thessalonians. The most popular and traditional position is that the Apostle Paul wrote both 1 and 2 Thessalonians. The taking up of this position has led several scholars to reverse the order of 1 and 2 Thessalonians, making 2 Thessalonians chronologically prior to 1 Thessalonians. The primary reason that Hugo Grotius reversed the order of the Thessalonian letters was the presence of the 'authenticating signature' (my term, not Grotius's) in 2 Thess. 3.17; for Grotius the presence of this authentication constituted a *magnum argumentum* against the traditional order of the Thessalonian letters. Grotius thus saw the authentication of 3.17 as speaking against the traditional order, since if the full force of 3.17 is maintained, and if 1 Thessalonians preceded 2 Thessalonians, then this 'authentication' by definition downgrades every Pauline letter which does not possess such an authentication. Hugo Grotius, acutely aware of rhetoric and rhetorical forms, was unable to believe that St Paul could have or would have written anything soon after 1 Thessalonians which would cast such doubt on its authenticity, especially when one reads the authentication of 3.17 in the context of 2.2, where the readers are exhorted not to be quickly shaken up by either 'spirit' or *logos* or 'a letter as from us'. These two verses taken together make it clear that a grand dialectic has been constructed by our author, a *crux* which forces the readers of 2 Thessalonians to choose between true Pauline teaching and letters (or perhaps a singular letter, namely 2 Thessalonians) and false Pauline teaching and letters. This dialectic is perfectly consistent with the rhetoric of this letter as a whole, as demonstrated in Chapter 3 of this study. The other side of the dialectic can be seen in 2 Thess. 2.15, where the readers are to hold fast to the true Pauline traditions, which are transmitted through *logos* and 'epistle'.

The attempts by several scholars who defend Pauline authorship for 2 Thessalonians to break the clear link between 3.17, 2.2, and 2.15, must be rejected for a number of reasons. First, to break the link between the 'authentication' of 3.17 and the topic of false epistle or epistles referred to in 2.2 (along with the topic of true epistle or epistles alluded to in 2.15) is to assume that our author is talking about different phenomena in these passages. A correct understanding of the rhetoric of this epistle must include an appreciation of the overarching dialectic that controls every aspect of this epistle. The alternatives posed include many different matters: true epistle of Paul *vs* false epistle of Paul (2.2; 2.15); those who believe the truth and will be saved *vs* those who rejoice in unrighteousness (2.12); the Man of Lawlessness with his parousia *vs* Christ and his parousia (2.9); the readers who are being afflicted with tribulation who are part of the elect *vs* those who are afflicting, whom God will pay back with affliction (1.5-9); the readers who are given a chance to find out God's eternal purposes through this epistle and to follow God's will *vs* the enemies of the readers (and of God) who do not know God and who do not obey the Gospel of our Lord Jesus (1.8); the prayer that Jesus and God will give the readers comfort and stability *vs* the doctrines which 'shake up' the readers (2.2,16-17; cf. 3.16); the example of Paul, who has the *ēthos* of an extremely hardworking man who refused to 'sponge' off anybody (though it would have been his prerogative to do so) *vs* the *ataktoi* ('disorderly ones') who are in 2 Thess. 3.6-10 defined as idlers; the peace which is God's gift to those who follow Pauline doctrine through this epistle (3.16) *vs* the feeling of being ashamed on the part of those who refuse to follow the right doctrine and are ostracized by this epistle's faithful readers (3.14-15); and finally, the overall *ēthos* of Paul as a faithful and good teacher and preacher *vs* the *ēthos* of the opponents of Paul and his mission, who are described in this letter as 'untoward', 'evil', and 'unfaithful' or perhaps more accurately, 'untrustworthy' (3.2).

To ignore any of these antitheses is to misunderstand the rhetoric of 2 Thessalonians, and particularly so if the conclusion of Chapter 3 of this study is correct, that 2 Thessalonians is an intentional document of deliberative rhetoric. Unlike epideictic rhetoric, which

typically uses the topics of praise and blame, and unlike judicial
rhetoric, where specific persons are prosecuted or defended on the
basis of their past behavior, in deliberative rhetoric the audience is
presented with crucial alternatives that will affect their future for
good or ill, depending on which choice the audience makes. The
antitheses that 2 Thessalonians sets before its readers are thus
entirely consistent with the *genus* of deliberative rhetoric and its
characteristic topics of advantage and honor. If the readers of this
epistle act honorably (that is, if they follow the true Pauline doctrine
of this epistle, and thus number themselves among the faithful and
stable followers of God, Jesus, and St Paul), they will do well in the
eyes of our author, and, given the apocalyptic consequences of
destruction by Jesus at the Last Judgment for the Antichrist and
those whom he will have deceived (2.11-12), they will also work to
their own eschatological advantage.

Another reason that the link between 2 Thess. 3.17, 2.2, and 2.15
must not be broken is because of the significant rhetorical function of
2.1-2. If the identification of 2.1-2 as the *partitio* of this letter is
correct, these verses should function either as a list of subjects to be
taken up in the two proofs in the *probatio* which follow, or they are
an identification of points of agreement and/or disagreement with
our author's adversaries. In 2 Thessalonians, the young Cicero's
distinction between the two types of *partitio* does not appear to be
operative, and here these two types of *partitio* are not mutually
exclusive.[2] Thus the *partitio* in this epistle serves to 'set up' or
introduce the proofs in two ways. First, the subjects of the two proofs
are introduced in 2.1-2, namely 'the coming of our Lord Jesus Christ
and our being gathered up with him' (2.1) and 'that you not be
quickly shaken in mind or excited' (2.2), referring to the two proofs
in 2.3-12 and 2.13-15 respectively. Second, the point of disagreement
is stated in 2.2, namely that there are those who 'by spirit or *logos* or
a letter as from us' who teach 'that the Day of the Lord has already
arrived'; and this very theology is the subject of the proof in 2.3-12,
which is a *refutatio* of the heretical theology. Since the *probatio* is
always the *sine qua non* of a rhetorical discourse, and since the
partitio coheres so well with the *probatio*, and since our epistle is so
short (by rhetorical standards if not by epistolary standards), it is
therefore extremely unlikely that the argument concerning true *vs*
false letters as related in the *partitio* can be unrelated to the
'authentication' of this letter as a true one in 3.17, nor can this topic

of letters be unrelated to the 'traditions which you have received from us, whether by *logos* or by our letter' (2.15), nor can it be unrelated to the order by the author to ostracize anyone who 'does not obey our teaching by means of epistle' (3.14). To assume that the 'authentication' of 3.17 does not relate to the overall argument concerning true and false letters—a topic so well attested all over this letter—is from a rhetorical point of view unacceptable, and especially in a document as short as 2 Thessalonians. To assume that these parts are not all constitutive of a whole is to cause confusion rather than to resolve it.[3]

Although from the headings in the canonical text, *Pros Thessalonikeis A'* and *Pros Thessalonikeis B'*, we cannot be sure which epistle was chronologically prior to the other (nor does the patristic attestation of these letters supply any clear information in this regard[4]), the reversal of the traditional order of 1 and 2 Thessalonians has been proposed by several scholars as a way of getting around problems with the Pauline authorship of 2 Thessalonians, assuming that Paul did write 1 Thessalonians. As discussed at the beginning of this study, Grotius reversed the order of the Thessalonian epistles primarily in order to preserve Pauline authorship of both letters, given the problem of the 'authenticating signature' in 2 Thess. 3.17. Other scholars have reversed the order for other reasons, such as Ferdinand Christian Baur and most recently John C. Hurd.[5] Baur's reasons for reversing the order seemed to stem from the definite doctrine of the Antichrist in 2 Thessalonians and the lack of anything 'for criticism to lay hold of' in 1 Thessalonians. Baur held that both Thessalonian letters were pseudonymous, but that 1 Thessalonians was literarily dependent on 2 Thessalonians.

For whatever reasons one might reverse the traditional order of 1 and 2 Thessalonians in order to preserve Pauline authorship, such a reversal fails to remove critical problems related to 2 Thessalonians; in fact, it creates new problems. First of all, the problems that are raised by 2 Thess. 3.17 are in no way removed by reversal of the order of 1 and 2 Thessalonians. By assuming that 2 Thessalonians were Paul's first letter, written in the 40s or 50s CE, we would still have the problem of Paul's warning his readers against forged Pauline letters, something that is doubly improbable, since there is no evidence that anyone would dare to (or would want to[6]) forge a Pauline letter during the lifetime of Paul, and since it is rhetorically unlikely that Paul would so erode his *ēthos* by even suggesting that letters 'as from us' could possibly be a source of false teaching; to do so would be a *faux pas* of the grandest sort on Paul's part. Also, the reversal of the order of the Thessalonian letters creates a new problem for the development of Paul's eschatology. Assuming that 2 Thessalonians is Paul's first letter and that 1 Thessalonians is his second letter, this alleged order creates the problem of Paul's first telling the Thessalonians that the Parousia of Christ will not be soon, after which Paul supposedly changes his mind and decides that the Parousia of Christ will be very soon indeed. Then, as Paul writes later epistles, Paul relapses into his earlier belief in the delayed Parousia, culminating in the belief in an extremely delayed Parousia as witnessed in his final letter, the Epistle to the Romans.

The reversal of the order of the letters to the Thessalonians, in order to retain Pauline authorship for both of them, makes the problem of 2 Thess. 3.17 and its words 'in every epistle' even more acute. To have Paul write 2 Thessalonians as his first extant letter, with the authenticating signature of 3.17 alleged to be 'in every letter' that Paul really wrote is even more absurd than to have this 'sign' in Paul's second letter, since it would be most strange for Paul to talk of 'every letter' if 2 Thessalonians were his first one to Thessalonika. The phrase 'in every letter' really can only make sense in an audience situation where multiple letters of Paul exist and are known to Christian readers; this is all the less likely, the earlier that 2 Thessalonians was written, assuming this was within the lifetime of Paul.

Although it is always dangerous for a scholar to assume that he or she knows what St Paul could not have said or meant, since the Apostle's writings possess an inexhaustible supply of surprises, certain alternatives do present themselves as more probable and others as less probable. Certainly the scenario of Paul's originally expecting an imminent Parousia of Christ, with his theology's then being revised to allow for the obvious delay of the Parousia as the traditional order of 1 and 2 Thessalonians would exhibit—followed then by other Pauline letters—has more internal probability than the scenario exhibited by the alleged order of 2 and then 1 Thessalonians. But before one becomes too confident about the direction in which St Paul's eschatology could or would develop, it would be more germane to ask larger questions about the eschatology of the two letters to the Thessalonians. Scholars who defend the hypothesis of

Pauline authorship of both these letters usually attempt to account for the great similarity of order and language, not by literary dependence of 2 Thessalonians on 1 Thessalonians, but by theorizing that the similarity of the two letters is due to St Paul's having written them chronologically quite close together; for Jewett, this meant a matter of a few weeks.[7] However well this might explain the striking similarities between these two letters, which are linguistically much closer to each other than any two other letters in the Pauline corpus, this explanation and its loyal adherents tend to run roughshod over the deep theological differences between the two letters, particularly in the realm of eschatology.[8] No matter who wrote either or both of these letters, it remains clear that their eschatologies are quite different.

Jewett seems to accept the conclusions of William Wrede (and others) that the many parallels in 1 and 2 Thessalonians point to a close connection between the text of 1 Thessalonians and the writing of 2 Thessalonians. Either Paul is the author of both letters, or the author of 2 Thessalonians used 1 Thessalonians as a literary source. The acceptance, however, of any part of Wrede's brilliant conclusions about 2 Thessalonians can only cause trouble for those who defend Pauline authorship of 2 Thessalonians. If Paul wrote both of them, the literary closeness between the two documents makes it most likely that they were both written within a short period of time of each other, since the repetition of so many words and phrases is likely to have been from memory, unless perhaps Paul kept a file copy of 1 Thessalonians for later reference. Hence, in order to take William Wrede's analysis of 2 Thessalonians seriously and as to explain the apparent theological differences between the letters, while defending Pauline authorship for both letters, it is necessary to explain these differences by some radical change within the life of either Paul or the Thessalonian church, and thus a change in Paul's relationship to them.

Jewett makes, I think, a relatively strong case for the possibility of such a radical crisis in the Thessalonian church through the use of indirect evidence. He brings much social and historical data into his argument that millenarian communities have historically exhibited some of the same characteristics as what he experimentally reconstructs as the congregational situation in Paul's church in Thessalonika.[9] He also has shown that further attention needs to be given to the church situation reflected in 1 Thessalonians. Probably because New

Testament scholarship is so strongly oriented towards the identification of opponents of Paul outside of his churches, it has tended to overlook the possibilities of tensions and conflicts within the churches themselves.[10] In order to sustain his thesis that Paul wrote 2 Thessalonians to counter a massive misunderstanding of 1 Thessalonians, Jewett constructs a model of the *ataktoi* as a group of millenarians within the Thessalonian church. Jewett claims that 2 Thessalonians reflects a situation in which

> the millenarian radicals were quoting Paul's teaching and writing to suport their contention that the Day of the Lord had already come. He summarized his earlier argument, quite naturally with a noticeable difference of tone. . . . The addition of new material in 2 Thessalonians, designed to clarify the nature of the eschatological signs that must precede the parousia, does not indicate a changed eschatological perspective on the author's part but rather the urgent need to demolish the belief that the parousia could be present while this evil age is still so clearly in evidence.[11]

1 Thessalonians, a letter in which the Thessalonians are roundly praised by Paul for the 'welcome' he had among them, and 'how you turned to God from idols, to serve a living and true God, and wait for his Son from heaven' (1 Thess. 1.9-10), presupposes and expounds faith in an extremely imminent Parousia of Christ. This Parousia will feature the resurrection of the dead, and 'those who have fallen asleep' (a euphemism for 'those who have died') will precede 'us who are alive' in the snatching up of believers into the clouds to meet the Lord Jesus in the air (1 Thess. 4.15-17). The imminently expected Parousia will indeed 'come like a thief in the night', so that none may accurately predict the time of Jesus' arrival (1 Thess. 5.2). Hence the events that will come upon the earth will be so sudden that they are characterized by Paul as a 'sudden destruction' and 'as travail comes upon a pregnant woman' (1 Thess. 5.3). Thus no apocalyptic signs of the time period *preceding* the Day of the Lord are given by 1 Thessalonians, even though eschatological timetables are a familiar part of apocalyptic literature in the New Testament,[12] because to give apocalyptic signs would be antithetical to the theology of 1 Thessalonians which holds that there are no recognizable signs before the Day of the Lord.

This eschatological material in stands in stark contrast to the eschatology of 2 Thessalonians, according to which, not only has the

Day of the Lord *not* already come, it also is believed not to be soon. This latter eschatology explains the long section in 2 Thessalonians where the author thanks God because of the readers' *hypomonē* (1.4) during the afflictions which the readers are suffering, which are, in fact, 'evidence of the righteous judgment of God, in order to make you worthy of the Kingdom of God, for which you indeed suffer' (1.5). The long thanksgiving section in 1.3-12, in which the sufferings of the elect are most prominent, strongly implies that the Parousia will be (or has been) a long time in coming. Further, in 2.3-12 we read an eschatological timetable, in which the eschatological signs are given that must appear *before* the Day of the Lord arrives. Moreover, 2 Thessalonians makes it clear that the teaching given in this letter is to be identified by the readers with the oral teaching of Paul when he was in Thessalonika: 'Do you not remember that when I was still with you I told you this?' (2.5). This is impossible to harmonize with 1 Thess. 5.2, where St Paul reminds the Thessalonians that 'you know *akribōs* (accurately) that the Day of the Lord is coming like a thief in the night', i.e. with no preceding signs of warning.[13] Moreover, the exhortation section in 3.6-13 takes up the subject of work; the readers are not to give up their jobs simply to wait for the coming Christ, or to allow other Christians to do the same: 'For even when we were with you, we gave you this command: If any one will not work, let him not eat' (3.10). Precisely because the Parousia will be a long time coming, the readers are finally exhorted, 'Brethren, do not be weary in welldoing' (3.13). Instead of the genuinely tolerant attitude of 1 Thess. 5.13-14, 'Be at peace among yourselves. And we exhort you, brethren, admonish the disorderly, encourage the fainthearted, help the weak, be patient with them all', we read in 2 Thess. 3.14, 'If anyone refuses to obey what we say in this letter, note that person, and have nothing to do with him, that he may be ashamed', even though there is a partial disclaimer of this acerbic attitude in 3.15. Indeed, the writer tells the readers that Pauline mission is being hindered by 'untoward and evil men, for not all are trustworthy' (3.2). On the contrary, as for the readers who follow Pauline doctrine, the holy Apostle is made to say quite pastorally, 'But the Lord is trustworthy; he will strengthen you and guard you from evil' (3.3).

The eschatological differences between the two epistles lead the reader ineluctably to the differences in pastoral *praxis* between them; both epistles are certainly apocalyptic, but the ways in which apocalyptic topics are used are significantly different. Hence, the change of eschatological perspective, through the addition of the apocalyptic timetable in 2 Thessalonians 2, along with other theological material related to endurance of hardships in ch. 1 and practical admonitions to work in ch. 3, must be seen as a major change in doctrine. Thus, if the literary similarities between the two epistles are to be explained by Paul's having written both of them, 2 Thessalonians rather soon after 1 Thessalonians (thus effectively throwing literary dependence out of court), the remarkable theological differences—at both the theoretical and practical levels—become all the more difficult to explain, which may be the reason why one of the most recent commentaries on the Thessalonian letters explains that the problem of the differences between the two letters is not really a problem.[14]

Historical criticism is not only the art of investigating what is possible; rather, it is much more the art of discovering and arguing in favor of the possibilities which are more or most probable. It does not seem likely to me that Paul, whose letters were considered 'weighty and strong' by his most rhetorically professional adversaries (2 Cor. 10.10), would have written what Jewett correctly terms a 'tightly organized deliberative letter'[15] which would yet make the colossal blunder of suggesting that letters purporting to be by the apostle might really be forgeries. Indeed, if the Thessalonian church had so radically misinterpreted Paul's apocalyptic language in 1 Thessalonians, and Paul later became aware of this, it remains unclear to me why a competent rhetorical writer would in response send a letter which uses many of the same words and phrases of the misunderstood letter, yet which reveals rather different theological presuppositions from those of 1 Thessalonians, yet at the same time warn against epistolary forgeries. My subjective impression of the rhetoric of 2 Thessalonians, in agreement with that of Hugo Grotius, is that it is certainly not primarily a particularly soothing or irenic letter. Like much other apocalyptic literature, it is highly inflammatory; indeed it seems considerably more apt to be misunderstood than 1 Thessalonians. Thus, the so-called *Ersatzcharakter* ('replacement character') noted by Heinrich Julius Holtzmann is much too mild a term to describe the rhetoric of 2 Thessalonians. It is rather a refutation of 'untoward', 'evil', and 'untrustworthy' enemies who, our author tells us, forged letters, 'believed the lie', and whom it is 'right' for God to repay with tribulation. Hence Holtzmann's description of the *Ersatzcharakter* of 2 Thessalonians (based as it was on his theory that the eschatological predictions in 1 Thess. 4.15, 17 *et passim* were unfulfilled, so that the author of 2 Thessalonians felt the need to replace these wrong predictions with 2 Thess. 2.1-12[16]) seems fundamentally ambiguous and should be abandoned. A much more precise term for 2 Thessalonians is 'refutation'.

The Hypothesis of Deuteropauline Authorship

Commentaries, monographs, and articles which accept the hypothesis that the historical Paul was not the direct author of 2 Thessalonians have suffered from another dilemma. It is easy enough to assert a nonpauline or Deuteropauline authorship for many epistles in the New Testament, but finding a scenario which adequately and positively explains why a later Paulinist most likely *did* write such an epistle is considerably harder to accomplish. In 1801, Johann Ernst Christian Schmidt suggested that 2 Thess. 2.1-12 was a Montanizing interpolation into an authentic Pauline letter, and other scholars have since expressed doubts about the same difficult section.[17] Although Ferdinand Christian Baur's overall theory concerning the nonpauline authorship of both the Thessalonian epistles was novel and creative in the extreme, it found no significant adherents, even in the Tübingen School, at least regarding the nonpauline authorship of 1 Thessalonians. Even William Wrede, who concluded that the 'Paul' of 2 Thessalonians was a different Paul from the one who was 'the enemy of Judaism, the Law, and the Old Testament' (Marcion's Paul), and who was also different from the 'Paul of orthodoxy' (the Paul of the Pastoral Epistles), was unable to place the 'Paul' of 2 Thessalonians in a historical situation.

> According to our epistle we now have, so to speak, yet another completely different Paul before us: the Paul who was the representative of a stormy eschatological expectation, in whose letters the weightiest matters were what he said of the End .... This 'Paulinism'—if we may really use such a term—remains for us an isolated fact. Whether it had a wider-reaching significance, and what this was, we do not know.[18]

Willi Marxsen made a very fresh suggestion in 1964 to the dilemma of the Thessalonian letters: he suggested that the people mentioned by 2 Thess. 2.1-2, who teach that 'the Day of the Lord has already come', were Gnostics.[19] Yet Marxsen could come no closer in an identification than that he felt that the letter was written soon after 70 CE.

Even though Willi Marxsen and William Wrede were in agreement that it is most likely that the 'Paul' who speaks in 2 Thessalonians is a different Paul than the Paul of the genuine Pauline epistles, even a different one from the Paul of 1 Thessalonians; they were still unable to come up with an identification of who this Paul was and what or whom this Paul spoke against. This is extremely ironic, because the Paul of 2 Thessalonians warns his readers not against just any Gnostic or gnosticizing heresy. 2 Thess. 2.2 makes it clear that the problem that our author polemicizes against is a problem *within* Pauline circles, since the sources of heresy are 'whether by spirit or by *logos* or by a letter as from us'. The enemy of the author of 2 Thessalonians is somebody who claims that this heresy is Paul's real theology, precisely by claiming authentication by 'spirit, *logos*, or a letter as from us', if not all three. If 2 Thess. 2.1-2 is indeed the *partitio*, as my analysis in the previous chapter of this study has argued, then the major issue in the interpreting 2 Thessalonians must be: Who speaks with Pauline authenticity? What does it mean to be authentically Pauline? If the heretics are Gnostics, they must be *Pauline* Gnostics who justify their theology by spreading it through letters which they wish to be accepted as Pauline.

Moreover, it is clear that this embarrassing situation of conflict among Paulinists could hardly have existed during the lifetime of Paul. But the New Testament exhibits for us an impressive literature of letters which evidently come from the postpauline period but which nevertheless claim to be Pauline letters. The Pastoral Epistles, which have no first century attestation, are certainly pseudonymous; and the most recent major monograph on them indicates that their rhetoric is directed against an heretical form of Paulinism, in which women had equal or nearly equal status as men.[20] Additionally, the Epistle to the Colossians and the Epistle to the Ephesians are by many mainline New Testament scholars considered doubtfully Pauline, particularly in recent New Testament introductions.[21]

A major difference between Ephesians and Colossians and the undisputed Pauline letters is the doctrine of eschatology. The important essays of Ernst Käsemann have made it clear that Paul's theology is eschatological through and through, and one may see this apocalyptic eschatology pretty clearly in every undisputed letter.[22]

The most recent major monograph on Paul's theology as a whole, J. Christiaan Beker's *Paul the Apostle: The Triumph of God in Life and Thought*, is a broad attempt to interpret Paul's theology with eschatology as the major strand running throughout.[23] There is a growing consensus among Pauline scholars of several persuasions that tends to see Paul's theology as deeply eschatological, with apocalyptic always being presupposed, in the undisputed epistles.[24] This being the case, Colossians and Ephesians seem to run exactly counter to this essential part of the theology of the undisputed letters.[25]

The Epistle to the Colossians

For the Pauline Christian who reads Colossians, the life of the earth and of the flesh is no more; the reader is exhorted,

> If therefore you have been raised with Christ, strive for the things which are above, where Christ is, seated at God's right hand. Think about things that are above, not things that are earthly. For you have died, and your life is hid with Christ in God. When Christ, who is our life, appears, then you too will appear with him in glory.[26]

Thus, Colossians argues, the real life of the Christian is already taking place now in heaven.[27] The believer is one who already lives in the eternal presence of God and Christ, hence the crucial importance of the Christ-hymn in Colossians, as well as the material that precedes it:

> May you be strengthened with every power, according to his glorious might, for all endurance and patience with joy, giving thanks to the Father, who has made us worthy to share the inheritance of the saints in light. He has rescued us from the dominion of darkness and transferred us to the Kingdom of his beloved Son, in whom we have redemption, the forgiveness of sins.[28]

To be a proper Pauline Christian is to be transferred *already* out of the earthly life and into the life of heaven, along with Jesus and God. 'Paul' also shares in this divine life, since Colossians does seem strongly to reflect traditions associated with the death of Paul. Paul is, in fact, seen as a kind of Christ-figure, the preeminent imitator of Christ in his sufferings: 'Now I rejoice in my sufferings for your sake, and in my flesh I complete what is lacking in Christ's afflictions for the sake of his body, that is, the Church ... ' (Col. 1.24). If this does indeed reflect the death of Paul (who evidently is seen to imitate the passion and death of Christ[29]), then it is possible to interpret Col. 2.5 in a broader way than it is normally interpreted: 'For though I am absent in body, yet I am with you in spirit, rejoicing and looking out for your order and the firmness of your faith in Christ'. Hence if Colossians does reflect the death of Paul,[30] then the 'Paul' who speaks in Colossians is a 'Paul' who speaks beyond the grave, and 'Paul's' presence is indeed in spirit only (or, 'in the Spirit only'), and this 'Paul' may indeed observe his disciples from his vantage point in heaven, to which he was 'transferred'. But how does this transferral take place? It takes place through a kind of cosmic incorporation into Christ, which is the subject of the Christ-hymn in Col. 1.15-20. In this hymn in particular, Christ is pictured and celebrated as the *makroanthrōpos*, a giant being whose body fills the whole world, a figure well investigated in the history of religions.[31] The *makroanthrōpos* is the creation of God, and in this being the fullness of deity dwells bodily (Col. 2.9; cf. 1.19). So this figure is connected with God through the act of God's creation, and he is identified with humanity through their redemption and 'transferral' into heaven:

> ... for in him were created all things, heavenly and earthly, visible and invisible, whether thrones or dominions or principalities or authorities—all things were created through him and for him. He is before all things, and all things cohere in him. He is the head of the body, the church; he is the beginning, the first-born from the dead, that in everything he might be preeminent.[32]

Hence the creation of the *makroanthrōpos* has already taken place and is a present reality.[33] Redemption, according to Colossians, takes place not so much through baptism and initiation into an earthly community as through *gnōsis* ('knowledge'). 'Paul' is here seen not as a fellow Christian and evangelistic missionary in the flesh; rather, 'Paul's' apostolic office is now seen as a teaching office, and 'Paul' teaches through the collection of Pauline letters,[34] hence 'Paul' speaks of his ministry and the church in this way:

> ... the church, of which I became a minister according to the divine administration which was given to me for you, to make the *logos* of God fully known, the mystery hidden for ages and generations but now made manifest to his saints.[35]

And what is this mystery? It is this: 'Christ in you, the hope of glory. Him we proclaim, warning every person and teaching every person in all wisdom, that we may present every person mature in Christ' (Col. 1.27-28). Evidently Christian maturity, according to Colossians, is the same thing as salvation, and these both take place by the teaching and learning of the mystery that Christ is a living reality within each believer, because each believer is quite literally a part of the Body of Christ—and this redemption is already a present reality, not reserved for the future. So it is not surprising that in this rather 'left-wing' branch of Deuteropauline Christianity, proper doctrine is of primary concern. Proper doctrine is that doctrine which contains *sophia* (wisdom); improper or heretical doctrine has no such wisdom to convey, by its very definition. Hence the Christian truly based in proper doctrine can rightly shun heresy, because it is only 'philosophy and empty deceit, according to the elemental spirits of the universe, and not according to Christ' (Col. 1.8). Thus the teaching that this empty doctrine gives is only part of the earthly sphere, not part of the heavenly sphere which must take precedence. Unlike the historical Paul (and also unlike 2 Thessalonians), the writer of Colossians teaches that Christ has already won the cosmic battle over the fleshly realm: 'He disarmed the principalities and powers and made a public example of them, triumphing over them in him' (Col. 2.15). Since the human sphere has been conquered by Christ already, the demands of the Law are no longer binding:'. . . having cancelled the bond which stood against us with its legal demands; this he set aside, nailing it to the cross' (Col. 2.14). Hence all earthly rules are null and void for the properly informed Pauline Christian, according to Colossians:

> Therefore let no one judge you concerning food and drink or concerning a festival or a new moon or a sabbath. . . . If together with Christ you died to the elemental spirits of the universe, why do you, as though you still lived in the world, submit to ordinances, such as 'Do not handle, Do not taste, Do not touch' . . . according to human precepts and doctrines?[36]

What ethical system there is for the readers of Colossians seems altogether simple, even simplistic:

> Put to death therefore the earthly in you. . . . Do not lie to each other, since you have put off the old person, with its practices and have put on the new person, which is being renewed in *epignōsis*

[knowledge, or 'superknowledge'] after the image of its creator, where there cannot be Greek and Jew, circumcised and uncircumcised, barbarian, Scythian, slave, free person; rather there is only Christ who is all and in all.[37]

According to the 'Paul' of Colossians, the new nature has already taken hold of Christians; they already live in heaven, since they are a part of the resurrected, exalted Body of Christ, which is a present and cosmic reality. Hence we can conclude that the eschatology of Colossians is an almost completely fulfilled or realized eschatology.[38]

The Epistle to the Ephesians

Ephesians, which evidently is related to Colossians through literary dependency,[39] has doctrines which are also quite similar to doctrines in Colossians. As early as 1933 Edgar J. Goodspeed argued cogently in favor of Ephesians' literary dependence on Colossians;[40] he also argued in favor of Ephesians' literary dependence on the other Pauline letters, which scholars found considerably less believable. Nevertheless, his work became a catalyst for later work on Ephesians, most notably that of the Englishman C. Leslie Mitton. In *The Epistle to the Ephesians: Its Authorship, Origin, and Purpose*, Mitton examined Goodspeed's theory in great detail, criticizing but essentially affirming Goodspeed's Ephesian hypothesis.[41]

Recent study of Ephesians has, with some notable exceptions,[42] taken Deuteropauline authorship for granted. Although the detailed studies of Percy and van Roon have argued in favor of Pauline authorship on a wide variety of grounds, particularly arguments on the basis of word usage,[43] many scholars nowadays accept Deuteropauline authorship of Ephesians primarily on form-critical and theological grounds, for reasons related to their understanding of the bases of Paul's theology. If apocalyptic eschatology is a crucial and nonoptional basis for Paul's theology, as held especially by Ernst Käsemann and as witnessed so well in Paul's undisputed letters (1 Thessalonians, Galatians, the Corinthian correspondence, Philippians, Philemon, and Romans), then Colossians and Ephesians can be understood to have come from Paul's pen only with great difficulty. Arguments in favor of Paul's authorship of Colossians and Ephesians also tend to ignore the strong signs therein of late first century Christianity as it structured itself for a long-term relationship with the Roman world,[44] developing a structure characterized by a

monarchical episcopate, increased reverence for apostles, increased
emphasis on sacraments, and, no less notably, an increasing
deemphasis on eschatology which is probably best explained by the
continued delay of the Parousia of Jesus. We need not assume an
absolute discontinuity of a combination of a 'high' understanding of
ministerial office, sacramental practice, and shifting views of
eschatology with Paul's own theology. Rather than trying to declare
such developments out of order within Pauline Christianity, we
should try to explain them historically.

For Ephesians, the real home of the Christian (and indeed, of the
church[45]) is 'in the heavenly places' (Eph. 1.3), where heavenly
blessings are found. Like Colossians, Ephesians teaches that
redemption is a present reality (Eph. 1.7) through the Christ-event.
Like Colossians, Ephesians functions so as to reveal a mystery to its
readers. For Colossians the mystery is 'Christ in you, the hope of
glory' (Col. 1.27), though in Ephesians there is the eternal plan of
God to unite all things, both in heaven and on earth, through Christ
(Eph. 1.10). Until the full inheritance is given, the Spirit is the
'guarantee' for the Christian (Eph. 1.13-14). For Ephesians, the
resurrection of Christ is coterminous with his enthronement in
heaven (Eph. 1.20) and exaltation over all earthly powers (Eph. 1.21-
22). The exaltation of Christ also implies the exaltation of the
believers to reign with Christ (Eph. 2.6). The major thrust of the
exaltation of believers is that it is understood by Ephesians to be in
the context of their unification, since the *makroanthrōpos* Christ is
the one new man who is the divinely crafted replacement *anthrōpos*
to take the place of the two previously defective *anthrōpoi*, with
which God has had nothing but trouble (Eph. 2.15; cf. Col 3.9).[46]
Through the death of Christ, the hostility between the Jew and the
Greek has come to an end (Eph. 2.14-16). Thus the redemption and
thus the unification that it necessitates are present realities, and
Christ and believers can be characterized by Ephesians as a temple
which grows together in the Lord, so as to be a 'dwelling place of God
in the Spirit' (Eph. 2.21-22). 'Paul's' chief office is to be a theologian,
that is, to be in charge of 'the administration of God's grace that was
given to me for you' (Eph. 3.2; cf. Col. 1.25), and that mystery was
made known to 'Paul' by revelation (Eph. 3.3), namely 'how the
Gentiles are fellow heirs, members of the same body, and partakers
of the promise of Christ Jesus through the Gospel' (Eph. 3.6). 'Paul'
is here understood as fulfilling that administrative task through his

'preaching', that is, through his writing of letters which contain the true doctrine (and thus *sophia*) of the mystery of Christ (Eph. 3.8).[47] The role of the church is to make known to the (other) heavenly beings the 'manifold wisdom of God' (Eph. 3.10). Since Paul and his sufferings are a part of the mystery of God's eternal purpose, the reader should not lose heart over Paul's sufferings.[48] Like Colossians, ethics in Ephesians is expressed in terms of death of the old nature *vs* resurrection and exaltation to a heavenly position and a new nature (Eph. 4.22-24), and, as Andreas Lindemann has pointed out, *not* in terms of a hope for a future salvation.[49]

Though the writer is of Ephesians is not completely consistent with his fulfilled eschatology,[50] nevertheless the overwhelming majority of statements do presuppose that a complete fulfillment of humanity through the Christ-event has taken place and is a present reality, in both Colossians and Ephesians. In neither of these similar doctrinal systems is there any indication that a Last Judgment is expected. Thus both these letters focus on the present reality of the Christ-event, and this is especially connected in both cases to the Spirit. Like 2 Thessalonians, both Ephesians and Colossians identify their doctrine with the doctrine of the historical Paul, and both of these letters imply that true Pauline doctrine comes to the readers of their letters through that letter itself.[51]

Conclusions

It is not difficult to see that a traditionally-minded, late first-century Pauline Christian who had internalized the words and theology of 1 Thessalonians could come to the justified conclusion that the authors of Colossians and Ephesians are indeed very plausible candidates for the identity of 'those who say, whether by Spirit or *logos* or a letter as from us, that the Day of the Lord has already arrived' (2 Thess. 2.2). In Colossians and Ephesians, we have real examples of pseudo- or Deuteropauline letters which teach a present fulfillment of eschatology, against whose doctrine it would not be at all unreasonable for the author of 2 Thessalonians to say, from his perspective deeply affected by apocalyptic elements in Paul's theology, that 'a letter as from us' teaches that 'the Day of the Lord has already arrived'.

Hence if 2 Thessalonians is seen as a Deuteropauline document among several other Deuteropauline documents, all of them vying for exclusive publishing rights for hitherto unknown letters of Paul, it then becomes possible better to understand the reasons for the paradox of the use of 1 Thessalonians by 2 Thessalonians along with the apparent eschatological incongruities between these two letters. The reasons that a 'right-wing' Paulinist such as the author of 2 Thessalonians could have to use 1 Thessalonians would then center on the fact that 1 Thessalonians would be thought by him to be an assuredly Pauline letter; hence, using phrases and whole sentences from it, as well as essentially following its order, could well result in the new letter's being accepted as an authentic letter of Paul; in fact it did. Not only does this letter claim to be an authentic Pauline letter (2 Thess. 1.1; 3.17), the letter also purports to identify its own teaching with that of the historical Paul when he was in Thessalonika founding the Thessalonian congregation (2 Thess. 2.5, 15). The letter sharply rebukes those who oppose its teaching, that is, 'Paul's' true teaching (2 Thess. 2. 2-3; 3.6-7, 10, 14). 2 Thessalonians goes so far as to imply strongly that the opponents of true Pauline doctrine will come to an undesirable end, since heretical believers are those who do not follow true doctrine (3.14; cf. 3.2 etc.).

Central to the eschatology of this letter is the delusion of heretics by God (2.9-12). Since the author of our letter addressed this to people for whom he was 'obliged to give thanks' (2 Thess. 1.3), which must mean that he believed that his readers would follow his doctrine and thus be saved (1.10; 2.3-17), it was possible to identify the enemies of our author's readers as enemies of Paul himself, whom it is right that God would pay back with tribulation (1.6) and vengeance, since these enemies are 'those who do not know God' and 'who do not obey the Gospel of our Lord Jesus' (1.8). Instead of false doctrine, which only 'shakes up' people (2.1) and is taught by 'wicked and evil men' who are 'untrustworthy' (3.2), our author offers his readers doctrinal stability (2.13-15), the result of which is consolation in the midst of persecution as well as 'eternal comfort and good hope through grace' (2.16), establishment in every good work and *logos* (2.17), and finally 'peace at all times in all ways' (3.16). Fully consistent with the *genus* of deliberative rhetoric and the crucial choices which it puts before its audience, the divine blessings for the readers (whoever they may be) are contingent upon their making the right choice (2 Thess. 1.11-12), in favor of our author's vision of Pauline Christianity. This is to say that the readers' eternal salvation depends upon their holding to the right doctrine and 'the traditions

which you were taught by us [= Paul], either by *logos* or by letter'
(2.15). If the Thessalonians are not (or do not become) *pistoi*
('faithful' or 'trustworthy'), it is clear that an undesirable eschatological
reward will come upon them (cf. 3.2), according to author's
theology.

In this study so far, it has been argued that our author argues
against Deuteropauline opponents on the battlefronts of *logos* and
epistle 'as from us'. Normally the words *hōs di' hēmōn* ('as from us')
are taken only with the words *di' epistolēs* ('through epistle'), so that
it is understood that the author of 2 Thessalonians opposes an
'epistle as from us'. Since doctrine, according to this epistle, is
inextricably linked with the topic of true *vs* false epistle, as has been
shown earlier in this chapter, it is likely that the phrase 'as from us'
can be plausibly construed to modify *dia logou* ('through oral
teaching') as well as 'through epistle'. In the concluding part of this
chapter, I suggest that the author of 2 Thessalonians may also be
opposed to doctrine which arises 'through the Spirit as from us',
which is to say that the phrase 'as from us' should be construed with
pneuma as well as with *logos* and 'epistle'.[52]

One very significant problem with the hypothesis of Pauline
authorship of 2 Thessalonians that is usually not discussed by its
defenders is the extremely difficult scenario of Paul's telling his
readers that 'Spirit' (whether 'a spirit' or 'the Spirit', meaning the
Holy Spirit) is a possible source of false doctrine in 2 Thess. 2.2.[53]
For St Paul to say such a thing, or even to suggest that the Spirit
would lead anybody into error, seems quite inconsistent with the
thought of the undisputed Pauline letters, to say the least. In
particular, if Paul were here suppressing prophetic utterance, he
would be in obvious contradiction to 1 Thess. 5.19, where Paul
advises, 'Do not quench the Spirit'. However, in both Colossians and
Ephesians the Spirit plays an important role, a role to which the
author of 2 Thessalonians seems to be opposed and, indeed, which he
wishes to refute. In Colossians, not only is *pneuma* the mode of
Christ's presence in the Church at the present time, it is also the
mode of *Paul's* presence with the readers, even though Paul is
admittedly 'absent in the flesh' (Col. 2.5).[54] Although, as Eduard
Schweizer points out, little is said about the Spirit in Colossians,[55]
what little there is there seems to indicate that it is the mode of presence of
Colossians' 'Paul' among his disciples. Moreover, there is a clear
connection made by Colossians between Spirit and prophetic

teaching in Col. 3.16, 'Let the *logos* of Christ dwell in you richly, as you teach and admonish one another in all wisdom, and as you sing psalms and hymns and spiritual songs (*ōdais pneumatikais*) with thankfulness in your hearts to God'.

In the Epistle to the Ephesians, however, a more prominent doctrine of the Spirit does emerge, as Rudolf Schnackenburg has pointed out.[56] For the writer of Ephesians, who also obviously writes in the name of Paul, the Spirit is the origin of unity in the Church, hence the passage, 'There is one body and one Spirit, just as you were called to the one hope that belongs to your call, one Lord, one faith, one baptism, one God and Father of us all, who is above all and through all and in all' (Eph. 4.4-6). Perhaps most importantly for the author of Ephesians, the Spirit is the basis for church order and church office, since the several offices in the church are gifts of the Spirit.[57] In fact, as Schnackenburg rightly points out, Eph. 4.1-16 instructs its readers at length about the role of the Spirit in the Church, although this has tended to be overshadowed by the Christology of Ephesians.[58] For Ephesians, the remedy for inappropriate behavior in the church and elsewhere seems to be 'being filled with the Spirit' (Eph. 5.17-20). And, just as both Ephesians and Colossians describe the Christian community as the Body of Christ which has cosmic dimensions, Eph. 2.22 reminds its readers that they themselves are a 'dwelling place of God in the Spirit'.

Many Hellenistic writers, including St. Paul, are fond of the epistolary cliché of constant, uninterrupted prayer, but for Ephesians this ceaseless prayer is to be 'in the Spirit' (Eph. 6.18). For Ephesians, the Word of God (*rhēma theou*) is the 'sword of the Spirit', part of the armor that the Christian needs to withstand the 'spiritual forces of wickedness in the heavenly places' (Eph. 6.10-17). In short, the fulfilled eschatology of Ephesians, like that of Colossians, requires a deity who actively participates in the present life of the Christian. For Colossians, more prominence is given to the identification of Christians as part of the *makroanthrōpos* Christ; however, in Ephesians, the present activity of God is more often explained by 'Spirit'.

If indeed 2 Thessalonians is a *refutatio* of a fulfilled eschatology propagated in the name of St Paul, the fact that *pneuma* is mentioned in 2 Thess. 2.1-2 as one of the sources of heresy that our author hopes will not 'shake up' his audience out of their wits, along with false *logos* and false Pauline epistle or epistles, is quite significant.

However, the author of 2 Thessalonians does not say directly that 'Spirit' brings heresy; rather, he only *suggests* that a *pneuma* 'as from us' is connected with false doctrine that threatens the stability of his readers. It is of great significance that the sources of true Pauline doctrine include, according to 2 Thess. 2.15, '[our] *logos*' and 'our epistle'—the Spirit is prominently absent.

I conclude that the author of 2 Thessalonians was outraged by the authoritative claims of his adversaries, as evidenced by their publishing ventures, which our author dismissed as forgeries, letters which St Paul never could have written. He thus retreated into the oldest and most authoritative writing of the Apostle that he possessed, 1 Thessalonians. Using this old letter as a model, our author made a powerful and well-argued reply, full of apocalyptic fire and yet chillingly cold, but clearly a polished piece of religious rhetoric. Hence, in the face of what our author believed to be the extreme writings of his adversaries, with whom he had all too much in common, our author could not remain tolerantly silent.

Chapter 5

CONCLUSIONS: THE LEGACY OF PAUL

If 2 Thessalonians is a document of polemical rhetoric from within Pauline Christianity which seeks to refute a form of fulfilled eschatology held by another branch of Pauline Christianity, it is then reasonable to conclude this study by suggesting the implications for the overall phenomenon of Paulinism, of which 2 Thessalonians and the controversy which evoked it are constitutive parts.

The History of Paulinism

In 1979, Andreas Lindemann published *Paulus im ältesten Christentum*.[1] This work, though not the first history of Paulinism,[2] has the advantage of being a modern study which takes into account many new advances in research and a variety of texts throwing light on the phenomenon of Pauline Christianity or Paulinism. Lindemann is able to give his readers a bird's-eye view of many parts of the complex phenomenon of how the image of the Apostle Paul was taken up in early Christianity up through Marcion. Lindemann examines several sources: First, the seven authentic letters of Paul (Romans, 1 and 2 Corinthians, Galatians, Philippians, Philemon, and 1 Thessalonians) are examined for traces of 'secondary expansions' or 'glosses', an examination implying that the collection and possible redaction of the Pauline letters involved the image of Paul. Then, Colossians and Ephesians are analyzed, since these are letters 'which arose under the pseudonym of Paul and have been brought together in ecclesiastical tradition as Pauline letters; they are looked upon by some exegetes as products of a theological school directly connected with Paul'.[3] The third category of sources of Paulinism for Lindemann includes 2 Thessalonians and the Pastoral Epistles.

Pseudonymous Pauline letters (which) are beyond these relatively early 'Deuteropaulines' are indeed 2 Thessalonians and the Pastorals; they are correctly assigned to the last part of the first century or the time around the turn of the century. Among all the Pseudopauline letters there is the image of Paul which is presupposed in these letters and partly, as is well known, is propagated by them, and which above all records the influence of a real theological Paul-tradition (which is to say, simply, the knowledge of the Pauline letters).

After these sources come the 'Pauline influence on the Gospels and Acts', along with the Apostolic Fathers, other church fathers, the Nag Hammadi texts, texts from Jewish Christianity, the early Apologists, and finally Marcion.[4] The analysis of the provenance of 2 Thessalonians in Chapter 4 of this study supports the idea that Colossians and Ephesians should be placed chronologically closer to Paul than 2 Thessalonians, since it is likely that 2 Thessalonians is a polemical reaction against those letters.

The subtitle of Lindemann's *Habilitationsschrift*, which in English would be 'The Image of the Apostle and the Reception of Pauline Theology in Early Christian Literature through Marcion', seems to be a programmatic description of his procedure, in that parts of the history of Pauline Christianity are presented in a rather linear fashion, even though the author disclaims a straight-line presentation of the history of Paulinism;[5] he does admit that it is better to speak of multiple images of Paul rather than a solitary image of Paul in the postpauline period.[6] Thus, the examples of early Christian literature examined by Lindemann are assessed as records of how Paul's image was developing in first- and early second-century Christianity.

Lindemann's learned and useful work, however, does not claim to be a complete history of Paulinism; it rather claims to set before the reader various images of St Paul in early Christianity. Unfortunately little consideration is given to the phenomenon of conflict *within* Pauline Christianity after Paul's death. Hence the evident polemic in many pieces of Deuteropauline literature, as well as in the 'glosses' or 'interpolations' in authentic Pauline letters, such as Rom. 16.17-20, are not really well explained by Lindemann. Thus Lindemann's book is basically an outline of the 'reception of Pauline theology' in the late first and early second centuries CE, rather than a description of the conflicts within Paulinism which evoked the literature of Paulinism.

In my opinion the major limitation of Lindemann's approach is that it tends to construe the writers of pseudopauline letters quite onesidedly as receivers of tradition, rather than as creators of traditions. This approach also tends to understand Pauline theology in primarily abstract and intellectual terms, rather removed from the conflicts of actual church life in the late first century and early second century CE. Yet in the Pastoral Epistles, there is a strong interest in portraying St Paul as one who promotes or even founds a very structured system of church offices, a structure perhaps not far removed from the structure we see promoted in the authentic letters of St Ignatius of Antioch.[7] The interest in church structure and polity which is so prominent in the Pastorals one also sees in Ephesians, and it may be reflected in Colossians,[8] while it seems to be absent in 2 Thessalonians. This brief example shows us that the meaning of church authority seems to constitute a significant part of the theologies of various pseudopauline writers. One can also see that the pseudopauline letters exhibit a great deal of diversity; in fact, almost the only things all the pseudopauline letters have in common is their agreement on Paul as an authority figure and their use of pseudonymity in order to claim that authority for themselves and their reading of what Paul's theology really was.[9] Just as the polemical rhetoric of the Pastoral Epistles is not well accounted for by a developmental scheme in which the presence of conflict between different brands of Paulinism is not dealt with as an extremely important factor, the apocalyptic polemic of 2 Thessalonians against other Paulinists implies an analogous phenomenon of conflict. The fact that several Deuteropauline writers believed it was to their advantage to use Paul's *ēthos* through pseudonymity in order to do polemical rhetoric suggests that the major conflicts which Deuteropauline writers were dealing with had not to do with enemies outside Pauline Christianity, but with theological adversaries who had conflicting claims to be within the realm of Paulinism. This implies that, at least in some communities in early Christianity, one's most dangerous theological enemies were theological thinkers and writers to whom one was closest,[10] particularly when one and one's enemies both claimed to have received the true doctrine from the same authority figure. Since in such a vexed situation nothing could be worse than too many Pauls around to confuse the faithful, the reactionary stance of the author of 2 Thessalonians becomes much more reasonable. Only such a heated and dangerous situation can explain why a pseudopauline author would go to the lengths that the writer of 2 Thessalonians did to provide a polished *refutatio* against those who promote their doctrine 'whether by Spirit, or by *logos*, or by a letter purporting to be from us' (2 Thess. 2.2), even though— quite paradoxically—2 Thessalonians is itself a pseudopauline letter.

In order to provide a more discussable picture of Deuteropaulinism, it seems useful to label the different Pauls who are identifiable within Deuteropauline Christianity.

The 'Paul of Heavenly Teaching'

This image of Paul is the Paul of Colossians, an image which was substantially accepted by the writer of Ephesians. The 'Paul of heavenly teaching' is a Paul who speaks from heaven, and he speaks most effectively to Christians who believe that they share with Paul the heavenly throne room and the eternal presence of God. For this Paul, the traditional eschatology of authentic Pauline letters is, generally speaking, outdated. Christian life is a phenomenon of the present, and the fellowship of the Christian believer with Christ is already quite complete. Thus, the admonitions by this Paul to his already-heavenly readers not to obey earthly regulations, since such regulations do not possess heavenly wisdom (Col. 2.20-23), are quite significant. If there are those in Pauline communities who resist the teaching authority of this heavenly Paul—and, perhaps, of his heavenly disciples—their opposition is based on an inadequate theology (the Paul of heavenly teaching maintains), which should be withstood. Any worship of Christ which the enemies of the heavenly Paul can perform must really be by those who do not rightly understand the divine cosmology and how Christ fits in it (Col. 1.15-20), as well as how Paul and other believers may participate in it (Col. 1.23; Eph. 3.2, etc.).[11] Paul's exaltation as heavenly by Colossians indicates one way in which the authority of his letters was grounded by part of the postpauline church.[12]

The 'Paul of Ecclesiastical Authority'

The Pastoral Epistles are themselves powerful documents of polemic, as Dennis MacDonald has recently shown.[13] MacDonald has argued that the provenance of the Pastoral Epistles is best explained by those documents themselves being documents of rhetoric which promote a set of images of Paul in order to oppose other images of Paul already present within Paulinism, images in the *Acts of Paul and Thekla* which portray Paul working amicably with Thekla, whom he treats as an equal or nearly equal colleague in ministry. Thus, in MacDonald's view, the Pastoral Epistles opposed such 'old women's tales' which had an interest in promoting women as colleagues with status equal to that of men in Christian ministry, *within* Pauline Christianity.[14]

The Paul of the Pastoral Epistles, who dominated the imaginations of the antiheretical Christian writers of the second and later centuries, is, in my opinion, much more of a 'realist' than the heavenly Paul of Colossians and Ephesians. The Paul of ecclesiastical authority is portrayed as delegating his authority to other Christians whom the Apostle apparently appoints or ordains to do certain sacred tasks for (Pauline) churches. The attempted standardization and regularization of ministries and ministers (which, as Elisabeth Schüssler Fiorenza has rightly argued, included its 'genderization'[15]) in the Pastoral Epistles implies that the charismatic authority which Paul both had and fought against was no longer tolerable by Christians who were loyal to this Paul.[16] Like the Paul of heavenly teaching, the Paul of ecclesiastical authority is opposed to false doctrine, but the Paul of ecclesiastical authority is much more vague as to what false doctrine is and what right doctrine is (1 Tim. 6.20, for example). This vagueness of doctrine coupled with a solidity of church order gives the Paul of ecclesiastical authority—and, clearly, his faithful disciples—tremendous power within the church because the authority of their church offices can be seen to allow the clergy to support or oppose almost any course of action they wish.[17]

The 'Paul of Apocalyptic Retaliation'

The Paul of 2 Thessalonians, whom I call the Paul of 'apocalyptic retaliation', appears to know nothing of the Paul of ecclesiastical authority, but these two Pauls are more similar than they are different. The 'canon' of the Paul of apocalyptic retaliation includes 1 Thessalonians, along with texts which portray God as visiting divine vengeance on sinners.[18] The Paul of apocalyptic retaliation is quick to specify which sinners God and the Lord Jesus will punish: those who believed 'the lie' and who did not believe in 'the truth', but rather who rejoiced in 'unrighteousness' (2 Thess. 2.11). This Paul is amazed that any so-called Christians would attempt to promote a false doctrine through false, forged Pauline epistles. The Paul who speaks in 2 Thessalonians realizes that the blessings of the heavenly realm are not yet in evidence, and thus he looks forward to 'rest' for himself (1.7) in the afterlife, and divine vengeance upon his enemies, which is, after all, only 'right' (1.6). The Paul of apocalyptic retaliation hopes that his readers will not be shaken up by a false, allegedly Pauline, doctrine (2.2); rather, he hopes that their Christian lives will be stable and predictable, at least doctrinally (2.15), if not emotionally (2.16) as well. Perhaps those who would attempt to 'shake up' Christians away from proper apocalyptic doctrine do so because they are already objects of a divine delusion (2.11); if so, this means that apocalyptic vengeance is already on its way. In any event, this Paul wishes his readers to make no mistake (2.3), for his enemies are 'untoward and evil people, for not all are trustworthy' (3.2). Should any Christians fall under the spell of the evil Paul, the Paul of 'heavenly teaching', who heretically teaches that human life is already over and that heavenly life has begun, the Paul of apocalyptic retaliation reminds his readers that the true Pauline example, shown in Paul's founding visit to Thessalonika, was an example of hard work (3.6-13). If anyone does not wish to observe this example so as to 'sponge' off other, hardworking, Christians, this Paul has a simple and quite practical solution, 'if anyone will not work, let him not eat' (3.10). But the Paul of apocalyptic retaliation is also a wise teacher; he realizes that faithful disciples do indeed get weary of doing good things (3.13). Yet his teaching blends mercy with severity: ostracism may be necessary for the most intractable sinners (3.14), but ostracism should be different from out-and-out war (3.15).

Conclusions

A polemical rhetorical universe dominated by conflicting images of Paul as the provenance of 2 Thessalonians was exactly what was proposed by William Wrede in 1903:

> From this Paul of orthodoxy, we make a clear distinction from the Paul constituted in a wholly different way by Marcion, the enemy of Judaism, the Law, the Old Testament. According to our epistle we now have, so to speak, yet another wholly different Paul before us: the Paul who was the representative of a stormy eschatological expectation, in whose letters the weightiest matters were what he

said of the End. . . . This 'Paulinism'—if we may really use such a term —remains for us an isolated fact. Whether it had a wider-reaching significance, and what this was, we do not know.[19]

The 'Paul of orthodoxy', in Wrede's words, was the 'Paul' of the Pastoral Epistles, who was different from the Paul of the genuine Pauline letters and different from the 'Paul' of 2 Thessalonians. For those who accept the full implications of Wrede's landmark study of 2 Thessalonians, the examination of the reception of Paul and his thought in Colossians, Ephesians, 2 Thessalonians, and the Pastorals, must not work with a solitary 'image of the Apostle' in mind, as the subtitle of Lindemann's work would seem to suggest; rather, the several pseudopauline letters only become really understandable when we posit that the theological and pastoral *ēthos* of Paul after his death can best be understood through *multiple* images,[20] and that the persons who promoted (or created) these multiple images were likely to have been in sharp conflict with one another—thus the multiple images. The indications are that each 'image' of the Apostle given by the various pseudopauline writers had its context in a situation of conflict.

Rhetorical criticism, oriented as it is towards discovery of the *ēthos*, *logos*, and *pathos* which make up persuasive texts, can deal very well with the presence of multiple Pauls in the postpauline era. Moreover, rhetorical criticism shows that the multiple Pauls cannot be reduced to a single image without an undesirable kind of 'melting down' or 'wearing away' of the sharp edges of the rhetoric of each letter, either in order to fit these letters into the theological patterns of the authentic letters of Paul (an unfortunate practice still perpetrated by many commentators) or in order to fit these letters into a wider scheme of the development of Pauline Christianity after the death of Paul,[21] a development which is by all accounts still insufficiently understood. In either case, to soften the sharp rhetorical edges of the pseudopauline letters results not in a plausible reading of the texts of these enigmatic letters; rather, it effects the creation of *different* texts, perhaps in order to avoid reading early Christian polemic as polemic, so as to perpetuate the myth of the earliest centuries of Christianity as a religious golden age,[22] or to perpetuate the myth of Pauline theology as a fundamentally unified or uniform phenomenon which could serve as a sort of 'canon within the canon'.[23] The unique perspective of 2 Thessalonians, together with its claim to speak for the 'real' Paul,[24] may well serve as the best corrective against both of these pervasive fallacies.

To analyze the rhetoric of the Deuteropauline and Pastoral letters does not denigrate their doctrinal or theological character. On the contrary, to read these pseudopauline letters in the context of the polemical rhetoric of refutation which they so richly contain makes their situational character—their unique integration into the theoretical and practical world of late first-century church life—come alive. When the situational character of these documents is properly understood, it will become possible to understand the theologies of Pauline Christianity more adequately, by way of investigating what sort of situational theologian each such writer really was. Thus, it may emerge that the writers of the pseudopauline letters were not merely forgers or weak epigones,[25] who must always be seen within the shadow cast by their master, but theologians in their own right who used a variety of theological sources and practiced rhetoric in creative ways for particular reasons, just as the historical Paul did.

NOTES

Notes to Chapter 1

1. H. Grotius, 'Annotationes in alteram epistolam ad Thessalonicenses', part of his *Annotationes in Vetus et Novum Testamentum* (1642) which is found in the Amsterdam edition (*Hugonis Grotii Operum Theologicorum* [Amsterdam: J. Blaev, 1679]), II/II, p. 948. See the lengthy history of scholarship on the authorship and provenance of 2 Thessalonians, with extensive English translations of early contributions to the debate in F.W. Hughes, 'Second Thessalonians as a Document of Early Christian Rhetoric' (Ph.D. dissertation, Northwestern University/Garrett-Evangelical Theological Seminary, 1984), pp. 1-74.

2. J.E.C. Schmidt, 'Vermuthungen über den beyden Briefe an die Thessalonicher', in: *Bibliothek für Kritik und Exegese des Neuen Testaments und ältesten Christengeschichte*, edited by Schmidt (Hadamar: Neue Gelehrten-buchhandlung, 1779-1803), II/3, 1801. This article was reprinted *in toto* in W. Trilling, *Untersuchungen zum zweiten Thessalonicherbrief* (Erfurter Theologische Studien, 27; Leipzig: St. Benno-Verlag, 1972), pp. 159-61, with modernized German spellings.

3. F.H. Kern, 'Über 2. Thess. 2,1-12. Nebst Andeutungen über den Ursprung des zweiten Briefs an die Thessalonicher', *Tübinger Zeitschrift für Theologie*, Jahrgang 1839, 2. Heft, pp. 145-214. See the summary and evaluation of Kern by J.E. Frame, *A Critical and Exegetical Commentary on the Epistles of St. Paul to the Thessalonians* (ICC; New York: Charles Scribner's Sons; Edinburgh: T.& T. Clark, 1912), pp. 40-41. R.A. Lipsius, 'Über Zweck und Veranlassung des ersten Thessalonicherbriefs', *TSK* 27 (1854), pp. 905-34, argued for Pauline authorship of 1 Thessalonians but did not directly comment on 2 Thessalonians. Later A. Hilgenfeld argued for Pauline authorship of 1 Thessalonians but against Pauline authorship of 2 Thessalonians in 'Die beiden Briefe an die Thessalonicher, nach Inhalt und Ursprung', *ZWT* 5 (1862), pp. 225-64.

4. F.C. Baur, *Paul, the Apostle of Jesus Christ*, second edn edited by E. Zeller, translated by A. Menzies, two volumes (London: Williams and Norgate, 1875-76). First edn was *Paulus, der Apostel Jesu Christi* (Stuttgart: Becher & Müller, 1845). Baur responded to Lipsius in 'Die beiden Briefe an die Thessalonicher: Ihre Echtheit und Bedeutung für die Lehre von der Parusie Christi', *Theologische Jahrbücher* 14 (1855), pp. 141-68. This article is translated by Menzies in Appendix III to Part II of Baur's *Paul, the Apostle of Jesus Christ*, II, pp. 314-40.

5. W. Wrede, *Die Echtheit des zweiten Thessalonicherbrief untersucht* (TU, n.F. 9/2; Leipzig: J.C. Hinrichs, 1903).
6. Wrede, *Echtheit*, pp. 70-71.
7. Wrede, *Echtheit*, p. 39.
8. Wrede, *Echtheit*, p. 70.
9. Wrede, *Echtheit*, p. 95.
10. A. von Harnack, 'Das Problem des 2. Thessalonicherbriefes,' *Sitzungsberichte der Königlich-Preussischen Akademie der Wissenschaften, philosophisch-historische Classe* 31 (Berlin: Königliche Akademie der Wissenschaften, 1910), pp. 560-78; M. Goguel, 'L'Énigme de la seconde épître aux Thessaloniciens', *RHR* 71 (1915), pp. 248-72; M. Dibelius, *An die Thessalonicher I-II, An die Philipper* (HNT, 3rd edn; Tübingen: J.C.B. Mohr [Paul Siebeck], 1937); E. Schweizer, 'Der zweite Thessalonicherbrief ein Philipperbrief?', *TZ* 1 (1945), pp. 90-105.
11. I.H. Marshall, *1 and 2 Thessalonians* (NCB; Grand Rapids: William B. Eerdmans; London: Marshall, Morgan & Scott, 1983); E. Best, *A Commentary on the First and Second Epistles to the Thessalonians* (Black's New Testament Commentaries; London: Adam & Charles Black, 1972); F.F. Bruce, *1 & 2 Thessalonians* (Word Biblical Commentary, 45; Waco: Word Books, 1982); B. Rigaux, O.F.M., *Saint Paul. Les Épîtres aux Thessaloniciens* (EBib; Paris: J. Gabalda, 1956).
12. W. Trilling, *Untersuchungen zum zweiten Thessalonicherbrief*; Trilling, *Der zweite Brief an die Thessalonicher* (EKKNT XIV; Zürich, Einsiedeln, Cologne: Benziger; Neukirchen-Vluyn: Neukirchener Verlag, 1980).
13. W. Marxsen, *Introduction to the New Testament: An Approach to its Problems* (Philadelphia: Fortress Press, 1968), pp. 37-44; *Der zweite Thessalonicherbrief* (Zürcher Bibelkommentare: Neues Testament 11/2; Zürich: Theologischer Verlag, 1982).

Notes to Chapter 2

1. Demosthenes, *Epistle* 1.3; English translation in Demosthenes, *Funeral Speech, Erotic Essay, Exordia, Letters*, translated by N.W. and N.J. DeWitt (LCL; Cambridge: Harvard University Press, 1949).
2. Isocrates, *Epistle* 1.2, to Dionysius.
3. Isocrates, *To Philip* 25-26.
4. On the relation of literary to oral rhetoric, see especially G.A. Kennedy, *Classical Rhetoric and its Christian and Secular Tradition from Ancient to Modern Times* (Chapel Hill: University of North Carolina Press, 1980), pp. 108-19. For a listing of patristic interpretations of this passage, see V.P. Furnish, *II Corinthians* (AB 32A; Garden City: Doubleday, 1984), p. 468. A more recent view of this passage and of the success of Paul's literary

rhetoric is found in W.A. Meeks, *The First Urban Christians: The Social World of the Apostle Paul* (New Haven: Yale University Press, 1983), p. 72, where Meeks comments: 'Some Corinthians have complained that, while Paul's letters are "weighty and strong," his "bodily presence is weak and [his] speech despicable" (2 Cor. 10:10). The claims which Paul makes just before this (10:1-6) are themselves claims about rhetorical ability, the ability "to take every thought captive." In 11:6 he admits to nonprofessional status (*idiotēs*) as an orator, but claims to possess *gnōsis*. That is an argument of the same order: Paul rhetorically boasts that he is no mere sophist'.

5. Augustine, *De doctrina Christiana* 4.12; English translation by D.W. Robertson, Jr, in: *On Christian Doctrine: St. Augustine* (Library of Liberal Arts; Indianapolis: Bobbs-Merrill, 1958).

6. Augustine, *De doctrina Christiana* 4.12.

7. Cicero, *De inventione* 1.1-5; *De oratore* 3.142-143; cf. 2.33 and 3.125.

8. Augustine, *De doctrina Christiana* 4.15.

9. C.G. Wilke, *Die neutestamentliche Rhetorik: Ein Seitenstück zur Grammatik des neutestamentlichen Sprachidioms* (Dresden & Leipzig: Arnold, 1843), p. IX.

10. Wilke, *Die neutestamentliche Rhetorik*, p. 469.

11. Wilke, *Die neutestamentliche Rhetorik*, p. 471.

12. Wilke, *Die neutestamentliche Rhetorik*, p. 475.

13. J. Weiss, 'Beiträge zur Paulinischen Rhetorik', in: *Theologische Studien. Herrn Wirk. Oberkonsistorialrath Professor D . Bernhard Weiss zu seinem 70. Geburtstage dargebracht* (Göttingen: Vandenhoeck & Ruprecht, 1897), pp. 165-274; the quotation is from p. 165.

14. Weiss, 'Beiträge', p. 167.

15. Weiss, 'Beiträge', p. 168.

16. Weiss, 'Beiträge', p. 184.

17. Weiss, 'Beiträge', pp. 184-98; the quotation is from p. 198.

18. Weiss, 'Beiträge', pp. 211-47.

19. Weiss, 'Beiträge', p. 247.

20. E. Norden, *Die antike Kunstprosa vom VI. Jahrhunderts vor Christus in die Zeit der Renaissance* (Leipzig: B.G. Teubner, 1898, 1913; repr. Darmstadt: Wissenschaftliche Buchgesellschaft, 1958).

21. Norden, *Die antike Kunstprosa*, p. 499.

22. Norden, *Die antike Kunstprosa*, pp. 498-510.

23. C.F.G. Heinrici, *Der zweite Brief an die Korinther, mit einem Anhang: Zum Hellenismus des Paulus* (MeyerK 6; 8th edn; Göttingen: Vandenhoeck & Ruprecht, 1900), pp. 436-58. On Heinrici and Norden, see H.D. Betz, *2 Corinthians 8 and 9: A Commentary on Two Administrative Letters of the Apostle Paul* (Hermeneia; Philadelphia: Fortress, 1985), p. 129 n. 2.

24. Heinrici, *Der zweite Brief an die Korinther*, p. 453.

25. R. Bultmann, *Der Stil der paulinischen Predigt und die kynisch-stoische*

Diatribe (FRLANT 13; Göttingen: Vandenhoeck & Ruprecht, 1910; repr. 1984).

26. In favor of understanding Pauline letters as rhetorical, with a review of patristic attitudes to Pauline rhetoric, there was a short statement by W.A. Jennrich, 'Classical Rhetoric in the New Testament', *Classical Journal* 44 (1948-49), pp. 30-32.

27. E.A. Judge, 'Paul's Boasting in Relation to Contemporary Professional Practice', *AusBR* 16 (1968), pp. 37-50.

28. E.A. Judge, 'The Early Christians as a Scholastic Community', *JRH* 1 (1960-61), pp. 4-15 and 125-37.

29. Judge, 'Paul's Boasting', p. 47, referring to his earlier article, 'The Early Christians as a Scholastic Community'.

30. Judge, 'Paul's Boasting', p. 42.

31. Judge, 'Paul's Boasting', p. 46.

32. H.D. Betz, 'The Literary Composition and Function of Paul's Letter to the Galatians', *NTS* 21 (1975), pp. 353-79.

33. W. Wuellner, 'Paul's Rhetoric of Argumentation in Romans', *CBQ* 38 (1976), pp. 330-51, reprinted in: *The Romans Debate*, ed. K.P. Donfried (Minneapolis: Augsburg Publishing House, 1977), pp. 152-74; Wuellner, 'Greek Rhetoric and Pauline Argumentation', in: *Early Christian Literature and the Classical Intellectual Tradition: In honorem Robert M. Grant*, ed. W.R. Schoedel and R.L. Wilken (Théologie historique, 53; Paris: Éditions Beauchesne, 1979), pp. 177-88.

34. H.D. Betz, *Galatians: A Commentary on Paul's Letter to the Churches in Galatia* (Hermeneia; Philadelphia: Fortress, 1979); for criticism of this work, see the penetrating review by W.A. Meeks in *JBL* 100 (1981), pp. 304-307; as well as W.D. Davies in *RelSRev* 7 (1981), pp. 310-18, reprinted in Davies, *Jewish and Pauline Studies* (Philadelphia: Fortress Press, 1984), pp. 172-88; see especially G.A. Kennedy, *New Testament Interpretation through Rhetorical Criticism* (Studies in Religion; Chapel Hill: University of North Carolina Press, 1984), pp. 144-52.

35. R. Jewett, 'Romans as an Ambassadorial Letter', *Int* 36 (1982), pp. 5-20. This article was written in preparation for Jewett's forthcoming two-volume commentary on Romans in the Hermeneia series, which will utilize rhetorical criticism as well as other types of criticism.

36. Betz, *2 Corinthians 8 and 9*, especially pp. 129-44. See the significant review of this book by Stanley K. Stowers in *JBL* 106 (1987), pp. 727-30.

37. M. Bünker, *Briefformular und rhetorische Disposition im 1. Korintherbrief* (Göttinger Theologischen Arbeiten, 28; Göttingen: Vandenhoeck & Ruprecht, 1984), which was presented in 1981 as a Dr.theol. dissertation in Vienna.

38. F. Siegert, *Argumentation bei Paulus gezeigt an Röm 9-11* (WUNT 34; Tübingen: J.C.B. Mohr [Paul Siebeck], 1985), which was originally

presented as a Dr.theol. dissertation in Tübingen; cf. C. Perelman and L. Olbrechts-Tyteca, *The New Rhetoric: A Treatise on Argumentation* (Notre Dame: University of Notre Dame Press, 1969).

39. K. Berger, *Formgeschichte des Neuen Testaments* (Heidelberg: Quelle & Meyer, 1984); cf. Berger, 'Hellenistische Gattungen im Neuen Testament', in: *Aufstieg und Niedergang der römischen Welt* II.25.2, ed. W. Haase (Berlin & New York: Walter de Gruyter, 1984), pp. 1031-432 and 1831-885; as well as Berger, 'Apostelbrief und apostolische Rede: Zum Formular frühchristlicher Briefe', *ZNW* 65 (1974), pp. 190-231.

40. For a recent collection of essays which were first presented in the Rhetorical Criticism section of the Society of Biblical Literature, most of which deal with the Hebrew Bible, see *Art and Meaning: Rhetoric in Biblical Literature*, ed. D.J.A. Clines, D.M. Gunn, and A.J. Hauser (JSOTS 19; Sheffield: JSOT Press, 1982). For recent methodological surveys, see V.K. Robbins and J.H. Patton, 'Rhetoric and Biblical Criticism', *Quarterly Journal of Speech* 66 (1980), pp. 327-50; R. Jewett, *The Thessalonian Correspondence: Pauline Rhetoric and Millenarian Piety* (Foundations and Facets: New Testament; Philadelphia: Fortress Press, 1986), pp. 63-68; F.W. Hughes, 'New Testament Rhetorical Criticism and its Methodology', paper presented in the Rhetorical Criticism section of the Society of Biblical Literature Annual Meeting, November, 1986 in Atlanta, Georgia; D.E. Knorr, 'The Rhetorical Consensus: A Proposed Methodology for the Study of Paul's Use of the Old Testament', paper presented at the Midwest regional meeting of the Society of Biblical Literature, February 20, 1986, at Andrews University; W. Wuellner, 'Where is Rhetorical Criticism Taking Us?', *CBQ* 49 (1987), p. 448-63.

41. A.J. Malherbe, 'Ancient Epistolary Theorists', *Ohio Journal of Religious Studies* 5 (1977), pp. 3-77.

42. Malherbe, 'Ancient Epistolary Theorists', p. 4.

43. 'Demetrius', *De elocutione* 223-35; see Malherbe, 'Ancient Epistolary Theorists', pp. 4-5, including notes 11-13. A convenient edition of *De elocutione* is that of W.R. Roberts, *Demetrius. On Style* ([bound together with Aristotle's *Poetics* and 'Longinus', *On the Sublime*] LCL; Cambridge: Harvard University Press, 1927). See also the text of *De elocutione* 223-35 with comments in K. Thraede, *Grundzüge griechisch-römischer Brieftopik* (Zetemata, 48; Munich: C.H. Beck, 1970), pp. 17-25.

44. H. Koskenniemi, *Studien zur Idee und Phraseologie des griechischen Briefes bis 400 n. Chr.* (Annales Academiae Scientiarum Fennicae, B 102/2; Helsinki: Suomalaien Tiedakatemie, & Wiesbaden: Otto Harrassowitz, 1956); on rhetoric and letters see especially pp. 19-34. Koskenniemi demonstrated on the basis of the epistolary handbooks that letters act to provide a means of furthering *philophronēsis* (goodwill between the writer and the readers, pp. 35-37), *parousia* (the presence of the writer with the

readers even though the writer is physically absent, pp. 38-42), and *homilia* (conversation between writer and readers , pp. 42-47). While it is certainly true that letters did and do provide a means of communication and commonality between writer and readers, this tells us more about the relation between form and intention of letters, but less about the relation between content and intention. In particular, epistolary theories such as this tell us little about how the argumentative structure of a particular letter works. For material that directly impacts the relation between the content of discourses and their intention, one must turn to rhetoric. That there was an overlap between rhetorical theory and letters is hardly surprising, primarily because the acquiring of goodwill and the furthering of relationships through were important concerns of rhetoricians. On the acquiring of goodwill, see below my discussion of the *exordium* in the rhetorical handbooks.

45. Malherbe, 'Ancient Epistolary Theorists', pp. 12-15.

46. Malherbe, 'Ancient Epistolary Theorists', p. 7.

47. Malherbe, 'Ancient Epistolary Theorists', p. 7; cf. H. Koskenniemi, 'Cicero über die Briefarten (genera epistularum)', *Arctos* n.F. 1 (1954), pp. 97-102.

48. Aristotle, *Ars rhetorica* 1.2.1.

49. J.L. White, *Light from Ancient Letters* (Foundations and Facets: New Testament; Philadelphia: Fortress, 1986).

50. White, *Light*, p. 3.

51. White, *Light*, p. 19; cf. White, 'Saint Paul and the Apostolic Letter Tradition', *CBQ* 45 (1983), pp. 433-44, and White, 'New Testament Epistolary Literature in the Framework of Ancient Epistolography', in: *Aufstieg und Niedergang der römischen Welt*, ed. W. Haase (Berlin & New York: Walter de Gruyter, 1984), II.25.2, pp. 1730-56.

52. White, *Light*, p. 187-220. The Greek text of these handbooks is found in V. Weichert, ed., *Demetrii et Libanii qui feruntur Typoi Epistolikoi et Epistolimaioi Charaktēres* (Leipzig: B.G. Teubner, 1910); English translation of them is found in Malherbe, 'Ancient Epistolary Theorists'.

53. White, *Light*, pp. 204-205; cf. 1 Thess. 4.13.

54. White, *Light*, pp. 206-208.

55. White, *Light*, pp. 205-206.

56. S.K. Stowers, *Letter Writing in Greco-Roman Antiquity* (Library of Early Christianity, 5; Philadelphia: Westminster, 1986). On letters and epideictic rhetoric see pp. 27-28; cf. Stowers's discussion of letter types and the *genera* of rhetoric on pp. 51-57. Elsewhere, Stowers emphasizes the need 'to compare Christian letters to the whole range of letters and to approach them with a knowledge of ancient epistolary and rhetorical theory (p. 23). On the following page, evidently concerning rhetorical criticism, Stowers writes, 'Recently there has been a revival of interest in the study of Greek and Roman rhetoric on the part of some New Testament scholars. A few

classical scholars have also taken an interest in the New Testament and
ancient rhetoric. Important beginnings have been made, beginnings that
often take up the leads of scholars from the beginning of this century who
were steeped in classical literature. It is too early, however, to speak of
definitive results or widespread agreement among researchers'.

57. Stowers, *Letter Writing*, p. 52.

58. Stowers, *Letter Writing*, p. 52.

59. H. Peter, *Der Brief in der römischen Literatur: Literargeschichtliche
Untersuchungen und Zusammenfassungen* (Abhandlungen der Königlichen
Sächsischen Gesellschaft der Wissenschaften, philologisch-historische Classe,
20/3; Leipzig: B.G. Teubner, 1901; reprint, Hildesheim: Georg Olms,
1965).

60. Peter, *Brief*, p. 14.

61. Peter, *Brief*, p. 19.

62. Aristotle, *Ars rhetorica* 3.12.2. On the effect of rhetoric on Latin prose
style, see A.D. Leeman, *Orationis Ratio: The Stylistic Theories and Practice
of the Roman Orators, Historians, and Philosophers*, two volumes (Amsterdam:
Adolf M. Hakkert, 1963) as well as the review of this work by G.A. Kennedy
in *American Journal of Philology* 87 (1963), pp. 237-41.

63. On Isocrates, see Kennedy, *Art of Persuasion in Greece*, pp. 174-203;
J.F. Dobson, *The Greek Orators* (London: Methuen, 1918; reprint, Chicago:
Ares, 1974), pp. 126-59; on the literary style of Isocrates, see Dionysius of
Halicarnassus, *Isocrates* 2-3, 11-20.

64. Quintilian, *Institutio oratoria* 9.4.19; Apollonius of Tyana, *Epistle* 19.

65. Cicero, *De oratore* 2.49; English translation is by E.W. Sutton and H.
Rackham, *Cicero. De oratore*, two volumes (LCL; Cambridge: Harvard
University Press, 1942).

66. Aristotle uses *psegein* for 'blame' rather than *memptein*.

67. Aristotle, *Ars rhetorica* 1.3.3 *et passim*. For a list of Pseudo-Demetrius'
twenty-one letter types, see White, *Light*, p. 203.

68. Aristotle, *Ars rhetorica* 1.10.1.

69. *Rhetorica ad Alexandrum* 1421b9.

70. J.J. Murphy, *Rhetoric in the Middle Ages: A History of Rhetorical
Theory from Saint Augustine to the Renaissance* (Berkeley: University of
California Press, 1974), p. 203, including notes 19 and 20.

71. Murphy, *Rhetoric in the Middle Ages*, p. 206.

72. *Dictaminum radii* 3.6, quoted from Murphy, *Rhetoric in the Middle
Ages*, p. 206.

73. Murphy, *Rhetoric in the Middle Ages*, p. 207.

74. Murphy, *Rhetoric in the Middle Ages*, p. 220.

75. Murphy, *Rhetoric in the Middle Ages*, pp. 224-25.

76. L. Rockinger, *Über Briefsteller und Formelbücher in Deutschland
während des Mittelalters* (Munich: J.G. Weiss, 1861); H. Rabe, 'Aus

Rhetoren-Handschriften: 9. Griechische Briefsteller', *Rheinisches Museum für Philologie* n.F. 64 (1909), pp. 284-309, with the literature referred to there.

77. Erasmus, *De conscribendis epistolis*, in: *Omnia opera Desiderii Erasmi Roterodami recognita et adnotatione critica instructa notisque illustrata* (Amsterdam: North Holland Publishing Co., 1971), with introduction and notes by J.-C. Margolin, I/2, pp. 153-579.

78. E.P. Parks, F.S.C., *The Roman Rhetorical Schools as a Preparation for the Courts Under the Early Empire* (Johns Hopkins University Studies in Historical and Political Science, 63/2; Baltimore: Johns Hopkins Press, 1945).

79. *De oratore* 1.86-87; 1.105.

80. Suetonius, *De grammaticis et rhetoribus* 4; Quintilian, *Institutio oratoria* 2.1.1-6.

81. Rabe, 'Aus Rhetoren-Handschriften', p. 289.

82. J.L. White, *The Form and Function of the Body of the Greek Letter: A Study of the Letter-Body in the Non-Literary Papyri and in Paul the Apostle* (second edn, corrected; SBLDS 2; Missoula: Scholars Press, 1972).

83. On the widening of a definition of the *Sitz im Leben* to include 'all typical situations of contact between text and social reality', see especially K. Berger, *Einführung in die Formgeschichte* (Tübingen: Francke Verlag, 1987), especially pp. 156-61 (quotation from p. 161). For a cogent critique of the limitations of form criticsm, see J. Muuilenburg, 'Form Criticsm and Beyond', *JBL* 88 (1969), p. 1-18, especially pp. 4-5.

84. Aristotle, *Ars rhetorica* 1.3.3.

85. *Ars rhetorica* 1.3.4.

86. *Ars rhetorica* 1.6.1 and 1.8.7.

87. On *De corona* in particular and on Demosthenes in general, see J.F. Dobson, *Greek Orators*, pp. 199-267, especially pp. 223-24; see also G.A. Kennedy, *Art of Persuasion in Greece*, pp. 206-36, especially pp. 232-36; L. Pearson, *The Art of Demosthenes* (American Philological Association Special Publications, 4; Chico: Scholars Press, 1981), pp. 178-99, with bibliography on pp. 1-3.

88. See Kennedy, *Art of Persuasion in Greece*, pp. 154-203.

89. R. Volkmann, *Die Rhetorik der Griechen und Römer in systematischer Übersicht* (2nd edn; Leipzig: B.G. Teubner, 1885), pp. 19-22.

90. See especially F. Solmsen, 'The Aristotelian Tradition in Ancient Rhetoric', *American Journal of Philology* 62 (1941), pp. 35-50 and 169-90.

91. *Ars rhetorica* 1.2.1.

92. A. Hellwig, *Untersuchungen zur Theorie der Rhetorik bei Platon und Aristoteles* (Hypomnemata 38; Göttingen: Vandenhoeck & Ruprecht, 1973); D.A.G. Hinks, 'Tria genera causarum', *Classical Quarterly* 30 (1936), pp. 170-76; F. Solmsen, 'Aristotelian Tradition in Ancient Rhetoric';

Volkmann, *Rhetorik der Griechen und Römer*; Kennedy, *Art of Persuasion in Greece*, pp. 26-82; on deliberative rhetoric see especially I. Beck, 'Untersuchungen zur Theorie des Genos Symbuleutikon' (Dr.phil. dissertation, University of Hamburg, 1970). For a collection of texts and fragments of rhetorical handbooks before Aristotle, see L. Radermacher, ed., *Artium Scriptores: Reste der voraristotelischen Rhetorik* (Sitzungsberichte der österreichischen Akademie der Wissenschaften, philosophisch-historische Klasse, 227/3; Wien: Rudolf M. Rohrer, 1951), as well as the older collection by L. Spengel, ed., *Rhetores Graeci* (Leipzig: B.G. Teubner, 1894).

93. J.H. Freese, 'Introduction' to *Aristotle. The "Art" of Rhetoric* (LCL; Cambridge: Harvard University Press, 1926), p. xxii.

94. *Ars rhetorica* 3.13.3.

95. Cicero, *De inventione* 1.19.

96. Cicero, *De partitione oratoria* 27.

97. Quintilian, *Institutio oratoria* 3.9.1.

98. *Institutio oratoria* 3.8.6.

99. *Institutio oratoria* 3.8.12.

100. *Institutio oratoria* 3.8.11.

101. See the introduction to the Loeb edition of [Cicero] *ad C. Herennium: De ratione dicendi (Rhetorica ad Herennium)* (LCL; Cambridge: Harvard University Press, 1954), translated and with an introduction by H. Caplan, pp. vii-xliv; especially on authorship, see pp. vii-xiv. *Partes orationis* quoted are found at *Rhetorica ad Herennium* 1.4.

102. Translation by E. Stump in *Boethius' De topicis differentiis* 1208C (Ithaca: Cornell University Press, 1978).

103. In H. Lausberg's *Handbuch der literarischen Rhetorik*, a similar but much more detailed chart is given which takes the rhetorical tradition even further forward, and Lausberg shows that the consensus concerning the *partes orationis* does continue well into the fifth century CE (Munich: Max Hueber Verlag, 1960; 2. Aufl., 1973); see the chart in I, p. 148. However, on the dangers of using Lausberg's learned *Handbuch* uncritically, see the review by A.E. Douglas, *Classical Review* n.s. 12 (1962), pp. 246-47.

104. D.E. Knorr, 'Rhetorical Consensus'.

105. *Ars rhetorica* 3.14.1.

106. *Ars rhetorica* 3.14.2.

107. *Ars rhetorica* 3.14.6.

108. Freese in *Aristotle. The "Art" of Rhetoric*, p. 431, note g.

109. *Ars rhetorica* 3.14.7.

110. Aristotle, *Ars rhetorica* 3.14.7.

111. *Ars rhetorica* 3.14.11, quoting Homer, *Odyssey* 7.327.

112. *Ars rhetorica* 3.14.12.

113. *Ars rhetorica* 3.14.11.

114. *De inventione* 1.20.

115. *De inventione* 1.20-21.

116. *De inventione* 1.26. On the securing of good will in Cicero's own practice, see P. Prill, 'Cicero in Theory and Practice: The Securing of Good Will in the *Exordia* of Five Forensic Speeches', *Rhetorica* 4 (1986), pp. 93-109.

117. *Institutio oratoria* 4.1.1.

118. *Institutio oratoria* 4.1.5.

119. *Institutio oratoria* 4.1.5; cf. *De inventione* 1.20: 'si eum benivolum, attentum, docilem confecerit'. Cf. also the statement in *Rhetorica ad Herennium* 1.6: 'ut adtentos ut dociles, ut benivolos auditores habere possimus', and 1.7: 'Quoniam igitur docilum, benivolum, adtentum auditorem habere volumus. . . '

120. *Ars rhetorica* 3.16.1.

121. *Ars rhetorica* 3.16.6.

122. *Ars rhetorica* 3.16.8.

123. *Ars rhetorica* 3.16.10.

124. *Ars rhetorica* 3.16.10.

125. *Ars rhetorica* 3.16.16.

126. *Ars rhetorica* 1.3.4.

127. *Ars rhetorica* 1.3.4.

128. *De inventione* 1.27.

129. *De inventione* 1.28.

130. *De inventione* 1.28.

131. *De inventione* 1.29.

132. *De inventione* 1.29.

133. *De inventione* 1.30.

134. *De inventione* 1.30.

135. *Institutio oratoria* 4.2.4.

136. *Institutio oratoria* 4.2.5.

137. *Institutio oratoria* 4.2.25-28.

138. *Institutio oratoria* 4.2.31-32.

139. *Institutio oratoria* 4.2.36-60.

140. *Rhetorica ad Herennium* 1.14.

141. *Rhetorica ad Herennium* 1.16.

142. Volkmann, *Rhetorik der Griechen und Römer*, pp. 167-69.

143. *De inventione* 1.31.

144. *De inventione* 1.31.

145. *De inventione* 1.31.

146. *De inventione* 1.32.

147. *De inventione* 1.32.

148. *De inventione* 1.33.

149. *Institutio oratoria* 4.5.1.

150. *Institutio oratoria* 4.5.22.

151. *Institutio oratoria* 4.5.22-23.

152. *Institutio oratoria* 4.5.26.
153. *Institutio oratoria* 4.5.27.
154. *Rhetorica ad Herennium* 1.17.
155. *Rhetorica ad Herennium* 1.17.
156. *Rhetorica ad Herennium* 1.17.
157. *Ars rhetorica* 3.13.4.
158. *Ars rhetorica* 3.17.3.
159. *Ars rhetorica* 3.17.4.
160. *Ars rhetorica* 3.17.5.
161. *De inventione* 1.34.
162. *De inventione* 1.78.
163. *Institutio oratoria* 5.Preface.5.
164. *Rhetorica ad Herennium* 1.18.
165. *Rhetorica ad Herennium* 3.8.
166. *Rhetorica ad Herennium* 1.4.
167. *Ars rhetorica* 3.13.4.
168. *Ars rhetorica* 3.19.1.
169. *Ars rhetorica* 3.19.1.
170. *Ars rhetorica* 3.19.1.
171. *Ars rhetorica* 3.19.4.
172. *De inventione* 1.98.
173. *De inventione* 1.98.
174. *De inventione* 1.100.
175. *De inventione* 1.100.
176. *De inventione* 1.107-109.
177. *Institutio oratoria* 6.1.1.
178. *Institutio oratoria* 6.1.1.
179. *Institutio oratoria* 6.1.1.
180. *Institutio oratoria* 6.1.9.
181. *Institutio oratoria* 6.1.11.
182. *Rhetorica ad Herennium* 2.47.
183. *Rhetorica ad Herennium* 2.47.
184. *Rhetorica ad Herennium* 2.47.
185. *Rhetorica ad Herennium* 2.50.
186. *De inventione* 1.109.
187. *Rhetorica ad Herennium* 2.50.
188. W.M.A. Grimaldi, S.J., *Aristotle, Rhetoric I: A Commentary* (New York: Fordham University Press, 1980), p. 80.
189. Aristotle, *Ars rhetorica* 1.3.5.
190. It is interesting that this ordering of the topics of rhetoric, in which advantage precedes and includes honor is exactly opposite the ordering of the young Cicero in *De inventione* 2.12; 2.156.
191. On *Synagōgē technōn* see Kennedy, *Art of Persuasion in Greece*, 13 including n. 9.

192. Kennedy, *Art of Persuasion in Greece*, pp. 70-72, especially n. 40.

193. Demosthenes' use of Isocrates is discussed in Plutarch's *Life of Demosthenes* 5.5.

194. Kennedy, *Art of Persuasion in Greece*, pp. 71f.

195. Kennedy, *Art of Persuasion in Greece*, p. 73.

196. Kennedy, *Art of Persuasion in Greece*, p. 74.

197. G. Norlin, *Isocrates* (LCL; Cambridge: Harvard University Press, 1929), II, pp. 4-5.

198. J.A. Goldstein, *The Letters of Demosthenes* (New York & London: Columbia University Press, 1968).

199. Kennedy, *Art of Persuasion in Greece*, p. 224.

200. G.A. Kennedy, 'Focusing of Arguments in Greek Deliberative Oratory', *TAPA* 20 (1959), pp. 131-38.

201. A. Weische, *Ciceros Nachahmung der attischen Redner* (Bibliothek der klassischen Altertumswissenschaften, n.F. 2/45; Heidelberg: Winter, 1972); C.W. Wooten, *Cicero's Philippics and their Demosthenic Model: The Rhetoric of Crisis* (Chapel Hill: University of North Carolina, 1983).

202. See the rhetorical analysis of *Epistle* 1 in Goldstein, *Letters of Demosthenes*, pp. 176-81; Goldstein's English translation of *Epistle 1* is found on pp. 204-207 of the same work.

203. See especially the discussion of exhortation (and dissuasion) in the pseudo-Aristotelian *Rhetorica ad Alexandrum* in connection with deliberative rhetoric, especially sections 1-2, which are 1421b7 to 1425b35 in the standard editions (see the edition by H. Rackham, *Aristotle. Rhetorica ad Alexandrum*, bound together with Aristotle's *Problems*, books 22-38 [LCL; Cambridge: Harvard University Press, 1957], pp. 275-305). In this system of rhetoric, speeches are divided into three kinds, deliberative, epideictic, and forensic, and these three kinds of rhetoric are divided into seven *eidē*, exhortation, dissuasion, eulogy, vituperation, accusation, defense, and investigation; deliberative rhetoric includes exhortation and dissuasion; cf. Aristotle, *Ars rhetorica* 1.3.3.

204. Several rhetorical letters which were written in the Hellenistic period, closer to the time of the New Testament, are found in C.B. Welles, ed., *Royal Correspondence in the Hellenistic Period: A Study in Greek Epigraphy* (New Haven: Yale University Press, 1934). Welles in his introduction, pp. xli-l, identifies letters 14, 22, 30, 36, 44, and especially 15 in his collection as rhetorical. These letters, mostly written as honorific communications from kings to subordinates, are generally epideictic in character. See Welles's translation and notes on letter 15, from Antiochus II to Erythrae, pp. 78-85. In this letter one can readily identify an exordium (including an epistolary prescript and a lengthy *captatio benevolentiae*), a narratio, a proof concerning the real reason for the letter (the king's grant of autonomy and tax-exemption to the city of Erythrae), an exhortation to the

city to act in ways consistent with its previous good record, and an ending greeting.

Notes to Chapter 3

1. The process of oral rhetorical patterns being used in literary discourses is summarized by W.R. Roberts, *Greek Rhetoric and Literary Criticism* (New York: Longmans, Green & Co., 1928); see also J. Martin, *Antike Rhetorik* (Handbuch der Altertumswissenschaft, II/3; Munich: C.H. Beck, 1974), pp. 6-7.

2. *Ars rhetorica* 1.2.3-4.

3. As found in Rom. 1.7b; 1 Cor. 1.2; Gal. 1.3; Eph. 1.2; Phil. 1.2; and Phlm 3; cf. 1 Tim. 1.2.

4. W.G. Doty, *Letters in Primitive Christianity*, pp. 29-30. K. Berger, 'Apostelbrief und apostolische Rede', argues that the greeting of 'grace and peace' has its best parallels in Judaism rather than in Greek epistolary literature.

5. Cicero, *De inventione* 1.22.

6. P. Schubert, *Form and Function of the Pauline Thanksgivings* (BZNW 20; Berlin: Alfred Töpelmann, 1939), p. 180.

7. R. Jewett, 'The Epistolary Thanksgiving and the Integrity of Philippians', *NovT* 12 (1970), pp. 40-53.

8. G.S. Holland, 'Let No One Deceive You in Any Way: 2 Thessalonians as a Reformulation of the Apocalyptic Tradition', in: *Society of Biblical Literature 1985 Seminar Papers*, ed. K.H. Richards (Atlanta: Scholars Press, 1985), pp. 327-41.

9. On the difficulty of reconciling this *Leidenstheologie* (theology of suffering) with Paul's theology of grace, see the recent article by J.M. Bassler, 'The Enigmatic Sign: 2 Thessalonians 1:5', *CBQ* 46 (1984), pp. 496-510, who identifies rabbinic parallels to this theology.

10. *Ars rhetorica* 3.17.4.

11. *Ars rhetorica* 1.3.4.

12. I. Beck, 'Untersuchungen zur Theorie des Genos Symbuleutikon', traces what can be known of deliberative rhetoric from presocratic sources through Aristotle.

13. See note 5 above.

14. *De inventione* 1.31-33; *Institutio oratoria* 4.5.1ff.

15. For a distinction between a 'day of wrath' and the 'day of our Lord Jesus Christ', see Holland, 'Let No One Deceive You', pp. 331-33; this position is well criticized by Jewett, *Thessalonian Correspondence*, pp. 99-100, including n. 44.

16. A significant grammatical problem is whether the words *hōs di' hēmōn*

('as from us') modify 'epistle' alone, or whether they should be construed with 'Spirit' and *logos* as well. In terms of Greek grammar, the construal of *hōs di' hēmōn* with all three instrumental clauses, *dia pneumatos* as well as *dia logou* and *di' epistolēs*, is reasonable in terms of the parallelism implied by the triple use of the preposition *dia*. The syntax of this verse could also be considered as an example of a mild form of hyperbaton; see H.W. Smyth, *Greek Grammar*, revised by G.M. Messing (Cambridge: Harvard University Press, 1956), p. 679, 3028, with examples. On the theological implications of the construal of 'as from us' with all three instruments, see the cautious note by J.B. Lightfoot, *Notes on Epistles of St. Paul*, ed. J.R. Harmer (London: Macmillan, 1918; repr. Grand Rapids: Baker Book House, 1980), pp. 109-10; see also the comments of Rigaux, *Thessaloniciens*, pp. 650-52, as well as the long roster of opinions collected by J.E. Frame, *Commentary*, pp. 247-48.

17.   This should be compared with the use of the same phrase in Gal. 6.7 and similar language in Col. 2.8; 1 Tim. 4.1-3; and Tit. 1.10.

18.   W. Bauer, *A Greek-English Lexicon of the New Testament and Other Early Christian Literature*, translated and adapted from the German by W.F. Arndt and F.W. Gingrich, 2nd edn revised and augmented by F.W. Gingrich and F.W. Danker (Chicago: University of Chicago Press, 1979), p. 98.

19.   Rigaux, *Thessaloniciens*, p. 654.

20.   H.D. Betz, 'Gottmensch II (Griechisch-römische Antike und Urchristentum)', in: *RAC*, ed. T. Klauser (Stuttgart: Anton Hiersemann, 1983), XII, columns 234-312.

21.   See the excellent historical studies by O. Mørkholm, *Antiochus IV of Syria* (Classica et mediaevalia, dissertationes 8; Copenhagen: Gyldendal, 1966); and J.A. Goldstein, *I Maccabees: A New Translation with Introduction and Commentary* (AB 41; Garden City: Doubleday, 1976), especially pp. 104-60; as well as the recent discussion in J.S. Pobee, *Persecution and Martyrdom in the Theology of Paul* (JSNTS 6; Sheffield: JSOT Press, 1985), pp. 21-23.

22.   See also the apocalyptic timetable in 2 Peter 3 and in the *Apocalypse of Peter*.

23.   The most notable recent study on the general outlook of apocalypticism is A.Y. Collins, *Crisis and Catharsis: The Power of the Apocalypse* (Philadelphia: Westminster Press, 1984), especially pp. 84-176. She argues that Revelation 'is a book that expresses anger and resentment and that may elicit violence' although the 'catharsis' given by the book of Revelation 'provided a feeling of detachment and thus greater control' (p. 171). That apocalyptic literature may presuppose a variety of world-views, see J .J. Collins, *The Apocalyptic Imagination: An Introduction to the Jewish Matrix of Christianity* (New York: Crossroad, 1984) as well as J.J. Collins, ed., *Apocalypse: The Morphology of a Genre* (Semeia 14; Missoula: Scholars Press, 1979).

24. O. Cullmann, 'Der eschatologische Charakter der Missionsauftrages und des apostolischen Selbstbewusstseins bei Paulus: Untersuchung zum Begriff des *katechon* (*katechōn*) in 2 Thess. 2,6-7', in Cullmann's *Vorträge und Aufsätze: 1925-1962* (Tübingen: J.C.B. Mohr [Paul Siebeck], 1966), pp. 305-36.

25. R.D. Aus, 'God's Plan and God's Power: Isaiah 66 and the Restraining factors of 2 Thess 2:6-7', *JBL* 96 (1977), pp. 537-53. The foregoing references to other scholars are found in Aus, pp. 537f.

26. In this connection, see also Job 4.9 (Septuagint) and Ps. 32.6 (Septuagint).

27. In apocalyptic contexts in early Christian literature, this occurs at *Didache* 16.4 and Rev. 13.13f.

28. As in *Didache* 16.4; *Ascension of Isaiah* 4.5; Mt. 7.21-23; as well as Mk 13.21-23 and its parallel Mt. 24.23-28.

29. On friendship letters as a genre see especially Stowers, *Letter Writing in Greco-Roman Antiquity*, pp. 58-70, 177.

30. As in Rom. 8.23; 11.16; 16.5; 1 Cor. 15.20, 23; 16.15; Jas 1.18; Rev. 14.4.

31. For example; 1 Thess. 2.12; 4.7; Rom. 8.20; cf. Eph. 4.1; Col. 1.10.

32. For examples of prayers in the *peroratio* of rhetorical speeches, see Demosthenes, *De corona* 324; *Second Philippic* 37; *Third Philippic* 76. Cicero often includes the oath *per deos immortales* in the *peroratio* of his speeches: *Pro Publio Quinctio* 96; *Pro Roscio Amerino* 153; *First Philippic* 38; *Second Philippic* 119; *Seventh Philippic* 25; cf. *Eighth Philippic* 29 (*O di immortales . . .*); cf. *Pro Roscio Comoedo* 50 (*Pro deum hominumque fidem!*).

33. See especially Cicero, *Thirteenth Philippic* 6-7, where the opinion of *Sapientia* (Wisdom) is considered as part of the *probatio*.

34. *Ars rhetorica* 3.19.1.

35. See Betz, *Galatians*, pp. 253-54.

36. Kennedy, *New Testament Interpretation through Rhetorical Criticism*, pp. 144-47; quotation is from p. 147.

37. See Betz, *Galatians*, pp. 253-54, including notes 8 and 15.

38. See Aristotle, *Ars rhetorica* 1.3.3.; Quintilian, *Institutio oratoria* 3.4.9; *Rhetorica ad Herennium* 1.2.2.; *Rhetorica ad Alexandrum* 1421b17-1425b35. Exhortation can also be seen at the ends of certain epideictic speeches, especially funeral speeches. Plato's *Menexenus* 246B-249E includes an exhortation of children to virtue (246D-247C), an exhortation against too much grief (247C-248C, 249C), and an exhortation to the city (248D); see also the exhortation of the funeral speech of Pericles in Thucydides, *History*, 2.44-46, concerning the appropriateness of grief. On the problem of the relation of philosophical exhortation to rhetoric, see M.D. Jordan, 'Ancient Philosophical Protreptic and the Problem of Persuasive Genres', *Rhetorica* 4 (1986), pp. 309-33; as well as A.J. Malherbe, *Moral Exhortation: A Greco-Roman Sourcebook* (Library of Early Christianity, 4; Philadelphia: Westminster Press, 1986), especially pp. 68-85 and 135-43.

39. D.E. Groh, Presidential Address at the Second Independent Conference of the North American Patristics Society (NAPS), 'Crisis in the Household: Affection and Defection in Early Christianity', given May 20, 1983, at Loyola University of Chicago.

40. As classically demonstrated by R.W. Funk, 'The Apostolic Parousia: Form and Content', in: *Christian History and Interpretation: Studies Presented to John Knox*, ed. W.R. Farmer, C.F.D. Moule, & R.R. Niebuhr (Cambridge: Cambridge University Press, 1967), pp. 249-68; see also K. Thraede, *Grundzüge griechisch-römischer Brieftopik*, pp. 148-61.

41. *Pace* R. Jewett, who in *The Thessalonian Correspondence: Pauline Rhetoric and Millenarian Piety* argues that Paul is convinced that what has happened in Thessalonika is that his own letter has been so massively misunderstood that he is forced to suggest that the source of heretical doctrine which his parishioners draw upon is a forged Pauline letter. Even if Paul was convinced of the existence of a forgery—which as far as anyone knows was unheard of during the life of Paul—it would be to Paul's rhetorical disadvantage to suggest that false Pauline letters were in circulation, because this would bring the authority of all other genuine Pauline letters into question. In all likelihood, Paul would not wish to do this, but to bring other interpretations of Pauline Christianity into question seems to be exactly what the author of 2 Thessalonians was doing. Also, the strongly epideictic rhetoric of 1 Thessalonians does not reflect nearly as serious a situation in Thessalonika as Jewett understands, in my opinion. On the rhetoric of 1 Thessalonians, see also B.C. Johanson, *To All the Brethren: A Text-Linguistic and Rhetorical Approach to 1 Thessalonians* (ConBNT 16; Stockholm: Almqvist & Wiksell International, 1987). For a parallel authentication in another pseudepigraphical letter, see Plato, *Epistle* 13: 'Let this greeting not only commence this letter but serve at the same time as a token that it is from me'.

42. See the recent work by D.K. Rensberger, 'As the Apostle Teaches: The Development of the Use of Paul's Letters in Second-Century Christianity' (Ph.D. dissertation, Yale University, 1981). Rensberger shows that both 'orthodox' and 'heretical' writers in the second century cited Paul and Pauline letters as authoritative.

Notes to Chapter 4

1. For a much more extensive review, see F.W. Hughes, 'Second Thessalonians as a Document of Early Christian Rhetoric', pp. 1-74.

2. Cicero, *De inventione* 1.31.

3. I.H. Marshall in *1 and 2 Thessalonians* and F.F. Bruce in his *1 & 2*

Thessalonians make the connection as weak as possible. Bruce (p. 164) comments: 'In the three extant letters where he does append his signature, drawing attention to the fact, there was probably some special reason for doing so. The reference in 2.2 to "a letter purporting to come from us" ... perhaps indicates what that special reason was in this letter; the name as well as the autograph would make this authentication doubly certain'. Marshall (p. 232) comments: 'But why is the attestation of authenticity present at all? On the assumption of genuineness, the possibilities commonly advanced are that Paul wished to enable his readers to distinguish this letter from other, inauthentic letters which may have been in circulation (cf. 2.2), or to stress the authenticity of this particular letter to any of the idlers who might try to discredit it. We have already seen that the former of these two possibilities is unlikely, and it seems more probable that Paul's purpose is to emphasise the authority and authenticity of this letter rather than to deny the authenticity of other alleged letters of his'.

4. The patristic attestations are examined in W. Bornemann, *Die Thessalonicher-Briefe* (MeyerK 10; 5th & 6th edn; Göttingen: Vandenhoeck & Ruprecht, 1894), pp. 319-20.

5. J.C. Hurd, Jr, paper presented at the December, 1983, Society of Biblical Literature meeting in Dallas, Texas, 'The Authenticity of II Thessalonians'. Previous scholars who have also reversed the order of 1 and 2 Thessalonians include J.C. West, 'The Order of 1 and 2 Thessalonians', *JTS* 15 (1914), pp. 66-74; J. Weiss, *Earliest Christianity: A History of the Period A.D. 30-150*, English translation ed. F.C. Grant, two volumes (Harper Torchbooks; New York: Harper, 1959), vol. I, pp. 213-23; T.W. Manson, 'St. Paul in Greece: The Letters to the Thessalonians', *BJRL* 35 (1953), pp. 438-47; R. Gregson, 'A Solution to the Problems of the Thessalonian Epistles', *EvQ* 38 (1966), pp. 76-80; C. Buck & G. Taylor, *Saint Paul: A Study in the Development of his Thought* (New York: Charles Scribner, 1969), pp. 140-45.

6. W. Marxsen, *Introduction to the New Testament*, pp. 42-44.

7. R. Jewett, 'Enthusiastic Radicalism', p. 200, comments: 'The second letter could very well have followed the first within a period of five to seven weeks'.

8. See, for example, E. Best, *A Commentary on the First and Second Epistles to the Thessalonians* (Black's New Testament Commentaries; London: Adam & Charles Black, 1972), pp. 55-58.

9. Jewett, *Thessalonian Correspondence*, pp. 111-32.

10. Jewett, *Thessalonian Correspondence*, p. 118.

11. Jewett, *Thessalonian Correspondence*, pp. 191-92.

12. Examples of apocalyptic timetables are found in Mk 13.3-37 and its parallels Mt. 24.4-36 and Lk. 21.8-36, as well as in the book of Revelation, *passim*; see especially Rev. 4.1, where the seer hears a voice 'speaking to me

122   *Early Christian Rhetoric and 2 Thessalonians*

like a trumpet', which says, 'Come up hither, and I will show you what must take place after this'. At the end of the visions, the seer is told in 22.6, 'And the Lord, the God of the spirits of the prophets, has sent an angel to show his servants what must soon take place'.

13. H.-H. Schade in his recent study, *Apokalyptische Christologie bei Paulus: Studien zum Zusammenhang von Christologie und Eschatologie in den Paulusbriefen* (Göttinger Theologische Arbeiten, 18; Göttingen: Vandenhoeck & Ruprecht, 1981), p. 178, also reached the conclusion that the eschatologies of 1 and 2 Thessalonians are irreconcilable.

14. I.H. Marshall, *1 and 2 Thessalonians*, pp. 37-38, comments: 'There is, then, no real disharmony between the two letters, and there is no problem about envisaging how the situation in Thessalonica may have led to the presentation of the two aspects of teaching in the two letters'.

15. Jewett, *Thessalonian Correspondence*, p. 82.

16. H.J. Holtzmann, 'Zum zweiten Thessalonicherbrief', *ZNW* 2 (1901), pp. 97-108, especially pp. 105-106.

17. P. Schmidt, *Der erste Thessalonicherbrief neu erklärt, nebst einem Excurs über den zweiten gleichnamigen Brief* (Berlin: Georg Reimer, 1885), p. 117: 'Auch abgesehen von II,1-12 trägt der Brief deutliche Spuren eines dem Apostel Paulus fremden Geistes'.

18. Wrede, *Echtheit*, pp. 70-71.

19. W. Marxsen, *Introduction to the New Testament*, pp. 38-39.

20. D.R. MacDonald, *The Legend and the Apostle: The Battle for Paul in Story and Canon* (Philadelphia: Westminster Press, 1983). On the Pastoral Epistles in general see N. Brox, *Die Pastoralbriefe* (RNT 7/2, 4th edn; Regensburg: Friedrich Pustet, 1969); M. Dibelius and H. Conzelmann, *The Pastoral Epistles: A Commentary on the Pastoral Epistles* (Hermeneia; Philadelphia: Fortress Press, 1972); C. Spicq, O.P., *Les Épîtres Pastorales*, Vol. I, 4th edn (EBib; Paris: J. Gabalda, 1969); A.T. Hanson, *The Pastoral Epistles* (NCB; Grand Rapids: William B. Eerdmans, and London: Marshall, Morgan & Scott, 1982).

21. For example P. Vielhauer, *Geschichte der urchristlichen Literatur*; E. Lohse, *The Making of the New Testament* (Nashville: Abingdon Press, 1983); E.D. Freed, *The New Testament: A Critical Introduction* (Belmont: Wadsworth Publishing Co., 1986); see especially the lucid treatment in H. Koester, *History and Literature of Early Christianity* (Foundations and Facets: New Testament; Philadelphia: Fortress Press; Berlin & New York: Walter de Gruyter, 1982), pp. 261-72. On the problem of the authorship of Colossians see A. Lindemann, *Der Kolosserbrief* (Zürcher Bibelkommentare, Neues Testament 10; Zürich: Theologischer Verlag, 1983), pp. 9-14. E. Schweizer, *The Letter to the Colossians* (Minneapolis: Augsburg Publishing House, 1982), pp. 15-26, lists arguments for and against Pauline authorship and cautiously concludes that Colossians is Deuteropauline; cf. his earlier article,

'The Letter to the Colossians—Neither Pauline nor Post-Pauline?' in: *Pluralisme et œcuménisme en recherches théologiques: Mélanges offerts au R. P. Dockx*, ed. Y. Congar, G. Dejaijve, & H. de Lubac (Paris and Louvain: Gembloux, 1976), pp. 3-16. Most recently M. Kiley, *Colossians as Pseudepigraphy* (Biblical Seminar, 4; Sheffield: JSOT Press, 1986), pp. 37-73, summarizes and argues against the various defenses of Pauline authorship for Colossians.

22. See especially Käsemann's essays, 'The Beginnings of Christian Theology', and 'On the Subject of Primitive Christian Apocalyptic', in Käsemann's *New Testament Questions of Today* (London: SCM Press; Philadelphia: Fortress Press, 1969), pp. 82-107 and 108-37.

23. J.C. Beker, *Paul the Apostle: The Triumph of God in Life and Thought* (Philadelphia: Fortress Press, 1980).

24. See especially Beker's chapter 9 in *Paul the Apostle*, 'Paul's Apocalyptic Theology: Apocalyptic and the Resurrection of Christ', pp. 135-81. L.E. Keck argues in 'Paul and Apocalyptic Theology', *Int* 38 (1984), pp. 229-41, that Paul makes a creative transformation of some parts of apocalyptic in his theology.

25. Recently P.J. Achtemeier has argued this with reference to the Pastoral Epistles, 'An Apocalyptic Shift in Early Christian Tradition: Reflections on some Canonical Evidence', *CBQ* 45 (1983), pp. 231-48. H. Koester commented in his *History and Literature of Early Christianity*, p. 264: 'Col 1.13 says that God "has transferred us to the kingdom of his beloved Son," using the past tense. In the genuine letters of Paul, however, which always say "kingdom of God" (never "kingdom of the Son"), the kingdom and one's participation in it are a matter of the future (e.g., 1 Cor 15.50). . . . In the interpretation of baptism, Col 2.12 and 3.1 state that the Christians have already died and have already risen with Christ. Paul, however, explicitly rejects this interpretation of baptism and consciously avoids speaking about rising with Christ as an event of the past (Rom 6.1ff; 1 Thess 4.14ff)'. For a view of the Pastoral Epistles as having an eschatology consistent with the genuine Pauline letters, see P.H. Towner, 'The Present Age in the Eschatology of the Pastoral Epistles', *NTS* 32 (1986), pp. 427-48.

26. Col. 3.1-4.

27. Cf. Kiley, *Colossians as Pseudepigraphy*, p. 67-68.

28. Col. 1.11-14.

29. See the sensitive discussion of Col. 1.24 in E. Schweizer, *The Letter to the Colossians* (Minneapolis: Augsburg Publishing House, 1982), pp. 99-106, as well as G. Schille, *Das älteste Paulus-Bild* (Berlin: Evangelische Verlagsanstalt, 1979), pp. 59-60.

30. In favor of a close relationship between Paul and the writer of Colossians, see Helga Ludwig, 'Der Verfasser des Kolosser-briefes—Ein Schüler des Paulus' (Dr.theol. dissertation, Georg-August-Universität Göttingen, 1974).

31. On the *Makroanthrōpos*, see E. Lohse, *Colossians and Philemon* (Hermeneia; Philadelphia: Fortress Press, 1971), p. 49, including n. 120; as well as K.M. Fischer, *Tendenz und Absicht des Epheserbriefes* (FRLANT 111; Göttingen: Vandenhoeck & Ruprecht, 1973), pp. 72-78, where Fischer discusses the idea of the Body of Christ as a 'Christian variant' of the *Makroanthrōpos* concept; see also W. Staerk, *Die Erlöserwartung in den östlichen Religionen: Untersuchungen zu den Ausdrucksformen der biblischen Christologie (Soter II)* (Stuttgart & Berlin: W. Kohlhammer Verlag, 1938), pp. 7-144.

32. Col. 1.16-18.

33. On the understanding of the *Makroanthrōpos*, also known as the *Urmensch* (primal man), in Colossians and Ephesians, see E. Käsemann, *Leib und Leib Christi: Eine Untersuchung zur paulinischen Begrifflichkeit* (BHT 9; Tübingen: J.C.B. Mohr [Paul Siebeck], 1933), pp. 138-59, where Käsemann compares the understanding of the Body of Christ in these Deuteropauline letters with that of the genuine Pauline letters. See also the earlier work by H. Schlier, *Christus und die Kirche im Epheserbrief* (BHT 6; Tübingen: J.C.B. Mohr [Paul Siebeck], 1930). Both Käsemann and Schlier argued that the understanding of the Body of Christ in Ephesians was strongly influenced by Gnosticism, though Käsemann even argued that Paul's own concept of the Body of Christ was basically Gnostic. On Käsemann's understanding of 'body', see R. Jewett, *Paul's Anthropological Terms: A Study of Their Use in Conflict Settings* (AGJU 10; Leiden: E.J. Brill, 1971), pp. 216-20.

34. Kiley, *Colossians as Pseudepigraphy*, pp. 103-104, argues that since the church in Colossae was noᵗ ᵗounded by Paul, 'The message is: Paul himself is not necessary to the foundation of a community which treasures his teaching'. This is perhaps another way of saying that Paul lives on through his letters.

35. Col. 1.24-26.

36. Col. 2.16, 20-21.

37. Col. 3.5, 9-11.

38. On the fulfilled eschatology of Colossians, see the comments of H. Koester, *History and Literature of Early Christianity*, p. 266. For a general study of realized eschatology, though not including that of Colossians or Ephesians, see D.E. Aune, *The Cultic Setting of Realized Eschatology in Early Christianity* (NovTSup 28; Leiden: E.J. Brill, 1972). See also the comments of J. Gnilka, *Der Kolosserbrief* (HTKNT X/1; Freiburg: Herder, 1980), pp. 11-12: 'Die Verkündigung des Evangeliums ist für Paulus das dem Ende zulaufende, eschatologische Ereignis, das den Menschen die endgültige Rettung im Gericht Gotte anbietet. Diese eschatologische Dimension ist im Kolosserbriefs gleichfalls nicht mehr vorhanden. Die Glaubenden sind Gerettete (2,11-13)'. Gnilka argues (p. 175), that Col. 3.4 is the only passage

in Colossians which has a coming Parousia of Christ in view.

39. See C.L. Mitton, *Epistle to the Ephesians*, especially pp. 55-82; more recently see H. Merklein, 'Paulinische Theologie in der Rezeption des Kolosser- und Epheserbriefes', in: *Paulus in den neutestamentlichen Spätschriften: Zur Paulusrezeption im Neuen Testament*, ed. K. Kertelge (Quaestiones disputatae, 89; Freiburg: Herder, 1981), pp. 25-69, especially pp. 25-27, for a recent discussion of the consensus regarding the authorship of Colossians and Ephesians and the dependence of Ephesians on Colossians; *idem*, 'Eph 4,1-5,20 als Rezeption von Kol 3,1-17 (zugleich ein Beitrag zur Pragmatik des Epheserbriefs'), *Kontinuität und Einheit: Für Franz Mussner*, ed. P.-G. Müller & W. Stenger (Freiburg: Herder, 1981), pp. 194-210. See also R. Schnackenburg, *Der Brief an die Epheser* (EKKNT X; Zürich, Einsiedeln, Cologne: Benziger Verlag, and Neukirchen-Vluyn: Neukirchener Verlag, 1982), pp. 26-30; as well as A. Lindemann, *Die Aufhebung der Zeit: Geschichtsverständnis und Eschatologie im Epheserbrief* (SNT 12; Gütersloh: Gerd Mohn, 1975), pp. 44-48.

40. E.J. Goodspeed, *The Meaning of Ephesians* (Chicago: University of Chicago Press, 1933).

41. C.L. Mitton, *The Epistle to the Ephesians: Its Authorship, Origin, and Purpose* (Oxford: Oxford University Press, 1951).

42. M. Barth, *Ephesians* (Anchor Bible 34-34a; Garden City: Doubleday, 1974).

43. E. Percy, *Die Probleme der Kolosser- und Epheserbriefe* (Skrifter utg. av Kungl. Humanistiska vetenskapssamfundet i Lund, 39; Lund: C.W.K. Gleerup, 1946); A. van Roon, *The Authenticity of Ephesians* (NovTSup 39; Leiden: E.J. Brill, 1974).

44. D.J. Harrington, S.J., *The Light of All Nations: Essays on the Church in New Testament Research* (Good News Studies, 3; Wilmington: Michael Glazier, 1982), pp. 60-78. See also E. Käsemann, 'Ephesians and Acts', in: *Studies in Luke-Acts: Essays presented in honor of Paul Schubert* (Nashville: Abingdon Press, 1966), pp. 288-97, where Käsemann comments: 'In the New Testament it is Ephesians that most clearly marks the transition from the Pauline tradition to the perspectives of the early Catholic era.... The entire letter appears to be a mosaic composed of extensive as well as tiny elements of tradition, and the author's skill lies chiefly in the selection and ordering of the material available to him' (p. 288).

45. See Schille, *Das älteste Paulus-Bild*, p. 62.

46. See Schnackenburg, *Der Brief an die Epheser*, pp. 306-309: 'Excurs: Die Kirche als Leib Christi'.

47. See Schnackenburg, *Der Brief an die Epheser*, pp. 33-34.

48. Eph. 3.13; this may be a reference to the death of Paul analogous to Col. 4.24, cf. Col. 2.5. On the theological meaning of the sufferings of Paul in Ephesians, see K.M. Fischer, *Tendenz und Absicht des Epheserbriefes*

(FRLANT 111; Göttingen: Vandenhoeck & Ruprecht, 1973), pp. 104-108.

49. A. Lindemann, *Die Aufhebung der Zeit*, p. 65.

50. See, for example, Eph. 4.13-16, 30; 6.13, which give veiled hints that a future fulfillment is in view. See especially Schnackenburg, *Der Brief an die Epheser*, p. 24: 'Vor allem ist hier die veränderte eschatologische Blickweise zu nennen. Die Parusieerwartung, die für Paulus und seine zwischen Heilsgegenwart und -zukunft angesiedelte, ihren Spannungscharakter ausmachende Theologie so bedeutsam ist, tritt im Eph noch stärker als in Kol (vgl. 3,4) zurück.' See also A. Lindemann, *Die Aufhebung der Zeit*, pp. 193ff., as well as G. Schille, *Das älteste Paulus-Bild*, p. 65.

51. Eph. 3.1-6; 3.14-16; cf. 3.8; 4.20-21; Col. 1.5-7; 4.7-8; 4.16.

52. B. Rigaux has no trouble construing 'as from us' with *logos* but confesses difficulty in construing the phrase with *pneuma*, *Thessaloniciens*, p. 651. F.F. Bruce (*1 & 2 Thessalonians*, 164) takes 'as from us' only with 'letter'. I.H. Marshall (*1 and 2 Thessalonians*, p. 187) says: 'It is more likely that the phrase goes with all three nouns, and that it refers not to whether the sources of teaching were truly Pauline but to whether the message attributed to Paul was a faithful representation of his teaching', which avoids the issue of authenticity. See Frame, *Commentary*, pp. 247-48.

53. By way of contrast, see the particularly fine discussion of the three sources of false doctrine in W. Trilling, *Der zweite Brief*, pp. 73-80.

54. Conversely, *pneuma* is also the method of 'Paul's' knowledge of the Colossians, and it is *pneuma* which has made the Colossians' love known to 'Paul', working through Epaphras, though this interpretation depends on what *en pneumati* in Col. 1.8 modifies, whether it is *ho dēlōsas* or *tēn hymōn agapēn*, and whether *en pneumati* should be taken instrumentally. On the problem of construing 'Spirit' here, see J. Gnilka, *Der Kolosserbrief*, pp. 37-38, including n. 56; see also E. Schweizer, *The Letter to the Colossians*, pp. 37-39.

55. E. Schweizer, 'Christus und Geist im Kolosserbrief', in *Christ and Spirit in the New Testament* (in honour of C.F.D. Moule), ed. B. Lindars, S.S.F., & S.S. Smalley (Cambridge: Cambridge University Press, 1973), pp. 279-313.

56. R. Schnackenburg, 'Christus, Geist und Gemeinde (Eph. 4.1-16)', in *Christ and Spirit in the New Testament* (see the previous note), pp. 279-96.

57. Eph. 4.7-12. This has been shown most recently on the Roman Catholic side by H. Merklein, *Das kirchliche Amt nach dem Epheserbrief* (SANT 33; Munich: Kösel, 1973), especially pp. 235-401 (see also Schnackenburg, *Der Brief an die Epheser*, pp. 33-34 and p. 79); and on the Protestant side by K.M. Fischer, *Tendenz und Absicht des Epheserbriefes*, pp. 109-72.

58. Schnackenburg, 'Christus, Geist', p. 279; cf. pp. 295-96. For a recent analysis of the Christology of Colossians, together with a summary of

problems associated with the reconstruction of the Christology of that letter's opponents, see F.O. Francis, 'The Christological Argument of Colossians', in: *God's Christ and His People: Studies in Honour of Nils Alstrup Dahl*, ed. J. Jervell & W.A. Meeks (Oslo: Universitetsforlaget, 1977), pp. 192-208.

Notes to Chapter 5

1. A. Lindemann, *Paulus im ältesten Christentum: Das Bild des Apostels und die Rezeption der paulinischen Theologie in der frühchristlichen Literatur bis Marcion* (BHT 58; Tübingen: J.C.B. Mohr [Paul Siebeck], 1979).

2. Earlier studies of Paulinism include O. Pfleiderer, *Paulinism: A Contribution to the History of Primitive Christian Theology*, translated by E. Peters, two volumes (London: Williams & Norgate, 1891), as well as E. Aleith, *Das Paulusverständnis in der alten Kirche* (BZNW 18; Berlin: Alfred Töpelmann, 1937), and A.E. Barnett, *Paul Becomes a Literary Influence* (Chicago: University of Chicago Press, 1941); see also the extensive bibliography in Lindemann, *Paulus*, pp. 408-32. A recent survey of issues involved in the history of Paulinism is C.K. Barrett, 'Pauline Controversies in the Post-Pauline Period', *NTS* 20 (1973-74), pp. 229-45.

3. Lindemann, *Paulus*, p. 13. On the understanding of Colossians as the product of an author directly connected with Paul, see H. Ludgig, 'Der Verfasser des Kolosserbriefes—Ein Schüler des Paulus'.

4. Lindemann, *Paulus*, p. 14.

5. Lindemann, *Paulus*, p. 6.

6. Lindemann, *Paulus*, p. 11.

7. See N. Brox, *Die Pastoralbriefe*, especially pp. 42-46; M. Dibelius and H. Conzelmann, *The Pastoral Epistles*, pp. 54-57; C. Spicq, O.P., *Les Épîtres Pastorales*, pp. 65-83; as well as H. von Campenhausen, *Ecclesiastical Authority and Spiritual Power in the Church of the First Three Centuries*, translated by J.A. Baker (Stanford: Stanford University Press, 1969), especially pp. 106-19. On Ignatius generally, see especially W.R. Schoedel, *Ignatius of Antioch: A Commentary on the Letters of Ignatius of Antioch* (Hermeneia; Philadelphia: Fortress Press, 1985).

8. E. Lohse, 'Christusherrschaft und Kirche im Kolosserbrief', *NTS* 11 (1964-65), pp. 203-16.

9. On pseudonymity, see especially W. Speyer, *Die literarische Fälschung im heidnischen und christlichen Altertum: Ein Versuch ihrer Deutung* (Handbuch der Altertumswissenschaft, I/2; Munich: C.H. Beck, 1971); N. Brox, *Falsche Verfasserangaben: Zur Erklärung der frühchristlichen Pseudepigraphie* (SBS 79; Stuttgart: Katholisches Bibelwerk, 1975); as well as Brox, 'Zum Problemstand in der Erforschung der altchristlichen Pseudepigraphie', *Kairos* 15 (1973), pp. 10-23; as well as the collection of

essays he edited, *Pseudepigraphie in der heidnischen und jüdisch-christlichen Antike* (Wege der Forschung, 484; Darmstadt: Wissenschaftliche Buchgesellschaft, 1977). For other views of pseudonymity, see B.M. Metzger, 'Literary Forgeries and Canonical Pseudepigrapha', *JBL* 91 (1972), pp. 1-24, as well as K. Aland, 'The Problem of Anonymity and Pseudonymity in Christian Literature of the First Two Centuries', *JTS* n.s. 12 (1961), pp. 39-49. On the use of pseudonymity in the Pastoral Epistles, see L.R. Donelson, *Pseudepigraphy and Ethical Argument in the Pastoral Epistles* (Hermeneutische Untersuchung zur Theologie, 22; Tübingen: J.C.B. Mohr [Paul Siebeck], 1986).

10. So argued D.E. Groh with reference to a Johannine school in 'Crisis in the Household'.

11. Compare the above discussion with the article by J. Gnilka, 'Das Paulusbild im Kolosser- und Epheserbrief', in: *Kontinuität und Einheit: Für Franz Mussner*, ed. P.-G. Müller & W. Stenger (Freiburg, Basel, Vienna: Herder, 1981), pp. 179-93; as well as K.M. Fischer, *Tendenz und Absicht der Epheserbriefes*, pp. 95-108.

12. C.M. Nielsen, 'The Status of Paul and his Letters in Colossians', *Perspectives in Religious Studies* 12 (1985), pp. 103-22.

13. D.R. MacDonald, *Legend*.

14. Macdonald, *Legend*, especially pp. 54-77; see also E.S. Fiorenza, *In Memory of Her: A Feminist Theological Reconstruction of Christian Origins* (New York: Crossroad, 1983), pp. 288-91, as well as my review article, 'Feminism and Early Christian History', *ATR* 69 (1987), pp. 287-99.

15. Fiorenza, *In Memory of Her*, pp. 294-315.

16. Fiorenza, *In Memory of Her*, pp. 286-88.

17. Compare the above brief discussion with the article by R.F. Collins, 'The Image of Paul in the Pastorals', *Laval théologique et philosophique* 31 (1975), pp. 147-73.

18. See the allusions to Isa. 53.3f. (Septuagint), Ps. 88.23 (Septuagint), Isa. 11.4 (Septuagint), and Dan. 11.36 in 2 Thess. 2.3, 4, 8.

19. W. Wrede, *Echtheit*, pp. 70-71.

20. M.C. de Boer, 'Images of Paul in the Post-Apostolic Period', *CBQ* 42 (1980), pp. 359-80.

21. The best example of this approach is O. Pfleiderer's *Paulinism*.

22. Against the idea that early Christianity should be looked upon as a golden age, see R.L. Wilken, *The Myth of Christian Beginnings: History's Impact on Belief* (Garden City: Doubleday & Co., 1971).

23. Against the idea that Paul or the Pauline corpus can be seen as the center of Holy Scripture, see E. Dassmann, *Der Stachel im Fleisch: Paulus in der frühchristlichen Literatur bis Irenäus* (Münster: Aschendorff, 1979), especially pp. 1-21, 313-20. For a survey of issues involved in understanding the meaning of the New Testament canon, see the essays edited by E.

Käsemann, *Das Neue Testament als Kanon* (Göttingen: Vandenhoeck & Ruprecht, 1970).

24. D.G. Meade, *Pseudonymity and Canon: An Investigation into the Relationship of Authorship and Authority in Jewish and Earliest Christian Tradition* (WUNT 39; J.C.B. Mohr [Paul Siebeck], 1986), p. 161, rightly refers to the epistolary framework of Ephesians and the Pastorals as 'part of the Pauline tradition itself, i.e. the characteristic Pauline method of mediating his apostolic presence'.

25. C.K. Barrett ('Pauline Controversies', p. 245) refers to the second-century interpreters of Paul as 'epigoni'.

BIBLIOGRAPHY

Commentaries on the Thessalonian Letters

Best, E., *A Commentary on the First and Second Epistles to the Thessalonians* (Black's New Testament Commentaries; London: Adam & Charles Black, 1972).

Bornemann, W., *Die Thessalonicherbriefe* (MeyerK 10; 5th and 6th edn; Göttingen: Vandenhoeck & Ruprecht, 1894).

Bruce, F.F., *1 & 2 Thessalonians* (Word Biblical Commentary, 45; Waco: Word Books, 1982).

Chrysostom, John, Saint, *The Homilies of S. John Chrysostom, Archbishop of Constantinople, on the Epistles of St. Paul the Apostle to the Philippians, Colossians, and Thessalonians*, English translation by W.C. Cotton, J. Ashworth, and J. Tweed (Oxford: John Henry Parker; London: J.G.F. & J. Rivington, 1843).

Dibelius, M., *An die Thessalonicher I-II. An die Philipper* (HNT 11; 3rd edn; Tübingen: J.C.B. Mohr [Paul Siebeck], 1937).

Dobschütz, E. von, *Die Thessalonicher-Briefe* (MeyerK 10; 7th edn; Göttingen: Vandenhoeck & Ruprecht, 1909; repr. 1974).

Ellicott, C.J., *A Critical and Grammatical Commentary on St. Paul's Epistles to the Thessalonians, with a Revised Translation* (Andover, Massachusetts: Warren F. Draper, 1881).

Frame, J.E., *A Critical and Exegetical Commentary on the Epistles of St. Paul to the Thessalonians* (ICC; New York: Charles Scribner's Sons, and Edinburgh: T. & T. Clark, 1912; 5th edn, 1960).

Friedrich, G., 'Der erste Brief an die Thessalonicher', & 'Der zweite Brief an die Thessalonicher', in: *Die Briefe an die Galater, Epheser, Philipper, Kolosser, Thessalonicher und Philemon*, Übersetzt und erklärt von Jürgen Becker, Hans Conzelmann, und Gerhard Friedrich (NTD 8, 14th edn; Göttingen: Vandenhoeck & Ruprecht, 1976).

Grayston, K., *The Letters of Paul to the Philippians and to the Thessalonians* (Cambridge: Cambridge University Press, 1967).

Grotius, H., *Annotationes in Vetus et Novum Testamentum*, in Grotius, *Operum Theologicorum* (Amsterdam: J. Blaev, 1679), II/III.

Krodel, G., '2 Thessalonians', in: *Ephesians, Colossians, 2 Thessalonians, The Pastoral Epistles* by J.P. Sampley, J. Burgess, G. Krodel, and R.H. Fuller (Proclamation Commentaries: The New Testament Witnesses for Preaching; Philadelphia: Fortress Press, 1978), pp. 73-96.

Lightfoot, J.B., *Notes on Epistles of St. Paul*, ed. J.R. Harmer (London: Macmillan, 1895; repr. Grand Rapids: Baker Book House, 1980).

Lünemann, G., *Critical and Exegetical Handbook to the Epistles of St. Paul to the Thessalonians*, translated by Paton J. Gloag (Critical and Exegetical Commentary on the New Testament; Edinburgh: T. & T. Clark, 1880).

Marshall, I.H., *1 and 2 Thessalonians* (NCB; London: Marshall, Morgan & Scott; Grand Rapids: William B. Eerdmans, 1983).

Marxsen, W., *Der erste Brief an die Thessalonicher* (Zürcher Bibelkommentare: Neues Testament, 11/1; Zürich: Theologischer Verlag, 1979).

132   *Early Christian Rhetoric and 2 Thessalonians*

—*Der zweite Thessalonicherbrief* (Zürcher Bibelkommentare, Neues Testament, 11/2; Zürich: Theologischer Verlag, 1982).

Masson, C., *Les deux épîtres de Saint Paul aux Thessaloniciens* (Commentaire du Nouveau Testament, 11a; Neuchâtel: Delachaux & Niestlé, 1957).

Milligan, G., St. *Paul's Epistles to the Thessalonians: The Greek Text with Introduction and Notes* (London: Macmillan, 1908).

Neil, W., *The Epistles of Paul to the Thessalonians* (MNTC 12; New York: Harper, 1950).

Plummer, A., *A Commentary on St. Paul's Second Epistle to the Thessalonians* (London: Robert Scott, 1918).

Reese, J.M., O.S.F.S., *1 and 2 Thessalonians* (New Testament Message, 16; Wilmington: Michael Glazier, Inc., 1979).

Rigaux, B., O.F.M., *Saint Paul. Les épîtres aux Thessaloniciens* (EBib; Paris: J. Gabalda; Gembloux: J. Duculot, 1956).

Schmidt, P., *Der erste Thessalonicherbrief, neu erklärt, nebst einem Excurs über den zweiten gleichnamigen Brief* (Berlin: Georg Reimer, 1885).

Staab, K., *Pauluskommentare aus der griechischen Kirche aus Katenenhandschriften gesammelt und herausgegeben* (NTAbh 15; Münster: Aschendorff, 1933).

—'Die Thessalonicherbriefe', pp. 7-63 in: *Die Thessalonicherbriefe, die Gefangenschaftsbriefe und die Pastoralbriefe*, by K. Staab & J. Freundorfer (RNT 7/2; 4th edn; Regensburg: Friedrich Pustet, 1965).

Trilling, Wolfgang, *Der zweite Brief an die Thessalonicher* (EKKNT XIV; Zürich, Einsiedeln, Cologne: Benziger Verlag; Neukirchen-Vluyn: Neukirchener Verlag, 1980).

Wohlenberg, Gustav. *Die erste und zweite Thessalonicherbrief* (Kommentar zum Neuen Testament, 12; 2nd edn; Leipzig: A. Deichert, 1909).

Articles and Monographs on the Thessalonian Letters

Aland, K., 'Das Ende der Zeiten. Über die Naherwartung im Neuen Testament und in der frühen Kirche', in: K. Aland, *Neutestamentliche Entwürfe* (TBü, Neues Testament, 63; Munich: Chr. Kaiser Verlag, 1979), pp. 124-82.

Alers, G.A., 'Ho katechōn en to katechon', *Theologische Studiën* 6 (Utrecht, 1888), pp. 154-76.

Andriessen, P., 'Celui qui retient la venue du Seigneur', *Bijdragen: Tijdschrift voor Filosofie en Theologie* 21 (1960), pp. 20-30.

Askwith, E.H., *An Introduction to the Thessalonian Epistles: Containing a Vindication of the Pauline Authorship of both Epistles and an Interpretation of the Eschatological Section of 2 Thess. ii* (London & New York: Macmillan, 1902).

Aus, R.D., 'Comfort in Judgment: The Use of the Day of the Lord and Theophany Traditions in Second Thessalonians 1' (Ph.D. dissertation, Yale University, 1971).

—'God's Plan and God's Power: Isaiah 66 and the Restraining Factors of 2 Thess 2:6-7', *JBL* 96 (1977), pp. 537-553.

—'The Liturgical Background of the Necessity and Propriety of Giving Thanks according to 2 Thess 1:3', *JBL* 92 (1973), pp. 432-38.

—'The Relevance of Isaiah 66:7 to Revelation 12 and 2 Thessalonians 1', *ZNW* 67 (1976), pp. 252-268.

Bahnsen, W., 'Zum Verständniss von 2. Thess. 2,3-12. Ein Beitrag zur Kritik des 2.ten Thessalonicherbriefes', *Jahrbücher für protes tantische Theologie* 6 (1880), pp. 681-705.

Bailey, J.A., 'Who Wrote II Thessalonians?' *NTS* 25 (1979), pp. 131-45.

Barnouin, M. 'Les problèmes de traduction concernant II Thess. ii.6-7', *NTS* 23 (1977), pp. 482-98.

Bassler, J.M., 'The Enigmatic Sign: 2 Thessalonians 1:5', *CBQ* 46 (1984), pp. 496-510.

Baur, F.C.,'*Die beiden Briefe an die Thessalonicher; ihre Echtheit und Bedeutung für die Lehre von der Parusie Christi*', *Theologische Jahrbücher* [Tübingen] 14 (1855), pp. 141-68. English translation by A. Menzies, pp. 314-40 of the following entry:

—*Paul, the Apostle of Jesus Christ, his Life and Work, his Epistles and his Doctrine: A Contribution to the Critical History of Primitive Christianity*, second edn, edited after the author's death by E. Zeller, translated by A. Menzies, two volumes (London: Williams & Norgate, 1875-1876).

Betz, O., 'Der Katechon', *NTS* 9 (1962-63), pp. 276-91.

Braun, H., 'Zur nachpaulinischen Herkunft des zweiten Thessalonicherbriefes', *ZNW* 43 (1952-53), pp. 152-56.

Burkeen, W.H., 'The Parousia of Christ in the Thessalonian Correspondence' (Ph.D. dissertation, University of Aberdeen, 1979).

Clemen, C., 'Paulus und die Gemeinde zu Thessalonike', *Neue kirchliche Zeitschrift* 7 (1896), pp. 139-64.

Cullmann, O., 'Le caractère eschatologique du devoir missionaire et de la conscience apostolique de S. Paul. Étude sur le "Katechon" de II Thess. 2,6-7', *RHPR* 16 (1936), pp. 210-45. German translation in the following entry:

—'Der eschatologische Charakter des Missionsauftrages und des apostolischen Selbstbewusstseins bei Paulus. Untersuchung zum Begriff des *katechon* (*katechōn*) in 2 Thess. 2,6-7', in: Cullmann, *Vorträge und Aufsätze 1925-1962*, ed. K. Fröhlich (Tübingen: J.C.B. Mohr [Paul Siebeck]; Zürich: Zwingli, 1966), pp. 305-36.

Dautzenberg, G., 'Tradition und Seelsorge aus Paulinischer Tradition. Einführung in 2 Thess, Kol, Eph', in: *Gestalt und Anspruch des Neuen Testaments*, ed. J. Schreiner (Würzburg: Echter-Verlag, 1969), pp. 96-119.

Day, P., 'The Practical Purpose of Second Thessalonians', *ATR* 45 (1963), pp. 203-206.

Dewailly, L.-M., 'Course et gloire de la Parole (II Thess III,1)', *RB* (1964), pp. 25-41.

—*La jeune eglise de Thessalonique* (Lectio Divina, 37; Paris: Cerf, 1963).

Donfried, K.P., 'The Cults of Thessalonica and the Thessalonian Correspondence', *NTS* 31 (1985), pp. 336-56.

—Review of W. Trilling, *Der zweite Brief an die Thessalonicher*, in: *TLZ* 109 (1984), pp. 200-201.

Eckart, K.-G. 'Der zweite echte Brief des Apostels Paulus an die Thessalonicher', *ZTK* 58 (1961), pp. 30-44.

Evans, R.M., 'Eschatology and Ethics: A Study of Thessalonica and Paul's Letters to the Thessalonians' (D.theol. dissertation, Basel, 1967).

Findlay, G.G., 'Recent Criticism of the Epistles to the Thessalonians', *Expositor* 6th series, 2 (1900), pp. 251-61.

Furfey, P.H., 'The Mystery of Lawlessness', *CBQ* 8 (1946), pp. 179-91.

Goguel, M., 'L'Énigme de la seconde épître aux Thessaloniciens', *RHR* 71 (1915), pp. 248-72.

Graafen, J., *Die Echtheit des zweiten Thessalonicherbriefs* (NTAbh 14/5; Münster: Aschendorff, 1930).

Gregson, R., 'A Solution to the Problems of the Thessalonian Epistles', *EvQ* 38 (1966), pp. 76-80.

Grimm, C.L.W., 'Die Echtheit der Briefe an die Thessalonicher', *TSK* 23 (1850), pp. 753-813.

Gruner, S., 'Besteht zwischen dem zweiten und ersten Briefe an die Gemeinde von Thessalonich eine literarische Abhängigkeit?' *Weidenauer Studien* 2 (1908), pp. 441-49.

Hadorn, W., *Die Abfassung der Thessalonicherbriefe in der Zeit der dritten Missionsreise des Paulus* (BFCT 24, 3/4; Gütersloh: C. Bertelsmann, 1919).

Harnack, A. von, 'Das Problem des 2. Thessalonicherbriefes', *Sitzungsberichte der Königlich Preussischen Akademie der Wissenschaften zu Berlin, philosophisch-historische Klasse* 31 (1910), pp. 560-78.

Hilgenfeld, A., 'Die beiden Briefe an die Thessalonicher nach Inhalt und Ursprung', *ZWT* 5 (1862), pp. 225-64.

Holland, G.S., 'Let No One Deceive You in Any Way: 2 Thessalonians as a Reformulation of the Apocalyptic Tradition', *Society of Biblical Literature 1985 Seminar Papers*, ed. K.H. Richards (Atlanta: Scholars Press, 1985), pp. 327-41.

—'The Tradition that You Received from Us: 2 Thessalonians in the Pauline Tradition' (Ph.D. dissertation, University of Chicago, 1986).

Hollmann, G., 'Die Unechtheit des zweiten Thessalonicherbriefs', *ZNW* 5 (1904), pp. 28-38.

Holsten, C., 'Zur Unechtheit des ersten Briefes an die Thessalonicher', *Jahrbücher für protestantische Theologie* 36 (1877), pp. 731-32.

Holtzmann, H.J., 'Zum zweiten Thessalonicherbrief', *ZNW* 2 (1901), pp. 97-108.

Hughes, F.W., 'Second Thessalonians as a Document of Early Christian Rhetoric' (Ph.D. dissertation, Northwestern University/ Garrett-Evangelical Theological Seminary, 1984).

Hurd, J.C., Jr, 'The Authenticity of II Thessalonians', paper presented at the December, 1983, Society of Biblical Literature meeting in Dallas, Texas.

Jewett, R., 'Enthusiastic Radicalism and the Thessalonian Correspondence', *Society of Biblical Literature: 1972 Proceedings* 1.181-232.

—*Paul's Anthropological Terms: A Study of Their Use in Conflict Settings* (AGJU 10; Leiden: E.J. Brill, 1971).

—*The Thessalonian Correspondence: Pauline Rhetoric and Millenarian Piety* (Foundations and Facets: New Testament; Philadelphia: Fortress Press, 1986).

Johanson, B.C., *To All the Brethren: A Text-Linguistic and Rhetorical Approach to I Thessalonians* (ConBNT 16; Stockholm: Almqvist & Wiksell International, 1987).

Kemmler, D.W., *Faith and Human Reason: A Study of Paul's Method of Preaching as illustrated by 1-2 Thessalonians and Acts 17,2-4* (NovTSup 40; Leiden: E.J. Brill, 1975).

Kern, F.H., 'Über 2 Thess. 2,1-12. Nebst Andeutungen über den Ursprung des 2. Briefs an die Thessalonicher', *Tübinger Zeitschrift für Theologie* 2 (1839), pp. 145-214.

Knox, J., 'A Conjecture as to the Original Status of II Corinthians and II Thessalonians in the Pauline Corpus', *JBL* 55 (1936), pp. 145-53.

Koester, H., 'Apostel und Gemeinde in den Briefen an die Thessalonicher', in: *Kirche: Festschrift für Günther Bornkamm zum 75. Geburtstag*, ed. D. Lührmann & G. Strecker (Tübingen: J.C.B. Mohr [Paul Siebeck], 1980), pp. 287-98.

Krentz, E., 'A Stone That Will Not Fit: The Non-Pauline Authorship of II

Thessalonians', paper presented at the December, 1983, Society of Biblical Literature meeting, Dallas, Texas.

—'Through a Prism: The Theology of 2 Thessalonians as a Deutero-Pauline Letter', paper presented at the November, 1986, Society of Biblical Literature meeting, Atlanta, Georgia.

Lake, K., 'II Thessalonians and Professor Harnack', *ExpTim* 32 (1920), pp. 131-33.

Lightfoot, J.B., 'The Church of Thessalonica', in: Lightfoot, *Biblical Essays* (London: Macmillan, 1893), pp. 251-69.

Lindemann, A., 'Zum Abfassungszweck des zweiten Thessalonicherbriefes', *ZNW* 68 (1977), pp. 35-47.

Lipsius, R.A., 'Über Zweck und Veranlassung des ersten Thessalonicherbriefs', *TSK* 27 (1854), pp. 904-34.

Malherbe, A.J., 'Exhortation in First Thessalonians', *NovT* 25 (1983), pp. 238-56.

Manson, T.W., 'St. Paul in Greece. The Letters to the Thessalonians', *BJRL* 35 (1953), pp. 428-47.

Michaelis, W., 'Der 2. Thessalonicherbrief kein Philipperbrief', *TZ* 1 (1945), pp. 282-85.

Milligan, G., 'The Authenticity of the Second Epistle to the Thessalonians', *The Expositor*, 6th series, 9 (1904), pp. 430-50 .

Orchard, J.B., 'Thessalonians and the Synoptic Gospels', *Bib* 19 (1938), pp. 19-42.

Peterson, R.J., 'The Structure and Purpose of Second Thessalonians' (Th.D. dissertation, Harvard Divinity School, 1968).

Ramsey, W.M., 'Dr. Milligan's Edition of the Epistles to the Thessalonians', *Expositor* 7th series, t. 7 (1969), pp. 1-17.

Reiche, J.G., *Authentiae posterioris ad Thessalonicenses epistolae vincidiae* (Göttingen: Vandenhoeck & Ruprecht, 1829).

Robinson, D.W.B., 'II Thessalonians 2,6: 'That which restrains' or 'That which holds sway'?' in: *Studia Evangelica II*, ed. F.L. Cross (TU 87; Berlin: Akademie-Verlag, 1964).

Rongy, H., 'L'authenticité de la seconde épître aux Thessaloniciens', *Revue Ecclésiastique de Liége* 21 (1929), pp. 69-79.

Schmidt, J.E.C., 'Vermuthungen über den beyden Briefe an die Thessalonicher', in: *Bibliothek für Kritik und Exegese des Neuen Testaments und älteste Christengeschichte*, ed. Schmidt (Hadamar: Neue Gelehrtenbuchhandlung, 1779-1803; II/3, 1801); repr. with modernized German spellings in W. Trilling, *Untersuchungen zum zweiten Thessalonicherbrief* (Leipzig: Erfurter Theologische Studien, 27; St. Benno-Verlag, 1972), pp. 159-61.

Schmithals, W., *Paul and the Gnostics* (Nashville: Abingdon Press, 1972).

—'Die Thessalonicherbriefe als Brief-kompositionen', in: *Zeit und Geschichte*, ed. E. Dinkler (Tübingen: J.C.B. Mohr [Paul Siebeck], 1964), pp. 295-315.

—'Zur nachpaulinischen Herkunft des zweiten Thessalonicherbriefes', *ZNW* 44 (1952-1953), pp. 152-56.

Schweizer, E., 'Der zweite Thessalonicherbrief ein Philipperbrief?' *TZ* 1 (1945), pp. 90-105.

—'Replik', *TZ* 1 (1945), pp. 286-89.

Stählin, W. 'Die Gestalt des Antichristen und das *katechon* (2 Thess. 2,6)', in: *Glaube und Geschichte: Festgabe Joseph Lortz*, ed. E. Iserloh & P. Manns (Baden-Baden: Bruno Grimm, 1958), II, pp. 1-12.

Stephenson, A.M.G., 'On the Meaning of *enestēken hē hēmera tou kyriou* in 2 Thessalonians 2,2', in: *Studia Evangelica IV* (TU, 102; Berlin: Akademie-Verlag, 1968), pp. 442-51.

Thompson, E.,'The Sequence of the Two Epistles to the Thessalonians', *ExpTim* 56 (1945), pp. 306f.

Trilling, W., 'Antichrist und Papsttum: Reflexionen zur Wirkungsgeschichte von 2 Thess. 2,1-10a', in: *Begegnung mit dem Wort: Festschrift für Heinrich Zimmermann*, ed. J. Zmijewski & E. Nellessen (BBB 53; Bonn: Hanstein, 1980), pp. 250-71.

—'Literarische Paulus-Imitation im 2. Thessalonicherbrief', in: *Paulus in den neutestamentlichen Spätschriften: Zur Paulusrezeption im Neuen Testament*, ed. K. Kertelge (Quaestiones disputatae 89; Freiburg, Basel, Vienna: Herder, 1981), pp. 146-56.

—*Untersuchungen zum zweiten Thessalonicherbrief* (Erfurter Theologische Studien, 27; Leipzig: St. Benno, 1972).

West, J.C., 'The Order of 1 and 2 Thessalonians', *JTS* 15 (1914), pp. 66-74.

Wrede, W., *Die Echtheit des zweiten Thessalonicherbriefs untersucht* (TU n.F. 9/2; Leipzig: J.C. Hinrichs, 1903).

Wrzol, J., *Die Echtheit des zweiten Thessalonicherbriefes* (Biblische Studien 19; Freiburg: Herder, 1916).

—'Sprechen 2 Thess. 2,2 und 3,17 gegen paulinischen Ursprung des Briefes?', *Weidenauer Studien* 1 (1906), pp. 271-89.

Zimmer, F. 'Zur Textkritik des zweiten Thessalonicherbriefes', *ZWT* 31 (1888), pp. 322-42.

Rhetoric, Rhetorical Criticism, and Related Studies

Allo, E.B., O.P., 'Le défaut d'éloquence et le style oral de Saint Paul', *RSPT* 23 (1934), pp. 29-39.

Aristotle. *The 'Art' of Rhetoric*, English translation by J.H. Freese (LCL; Cambridge: Harvard University Press, 1926).

Augustine. *On Christian Doctrine*, English translation by D.W. Robinson, Jr (Library of Liberal Arts; Indianapolis: Bobbs-Merrill, 1958).

Beck, I., 'Untersuchungen zur Theorie des Genos Symbuleutikon' (Dr.phil. dissertation, University of Hamburg, 1970).

Berger, K., 'Apostelbrief und apostolische Rede: Zum Formular fürhchristlicher Briefe', *ZNW* 65 (1974), pp. 190-231.

—*Einführung in die Formgeschichte* (Tübingen: Franke Verlag, 1987).

—*Formgeschichte des Neuen Testaments* (Heidelberg: Quelle & Meyer, 1984).

—'Hellenistische Gattungen im Neuen Testament', in: *Aufstieg und Niedergang der römischen Welt* II.25.2, ed. Wolfgang Haase (Berlin & New York: Walter de Gruyter, 1984), pp. 1031-1432, 1831-1885.

Betz, H.D., *2 Corinthians 8 and 9: A Commentary on Two Administrative Letters of the Apostle Paul* (Hermeneia: Philadelphia: Fortress Press, 1985).

—*Galatians: A Commentary on Paul's Letter to the Churches in Galatia* (Hermeneia; Philadelphia: Fortress Press, 1979).

—'The Literary Composition and Function of Paul's Letter to the Galatians', *NTS* 21 (1975), pp. 353-79.

Boethius' *De Topicis Differentiis*. English translation, with essays on the text, by Eleonore Stump (Ithaca: Cornell University Press, 1978).

Brock, B.L., & R.L. Scott, eds., *Methods of Rhetorical Criticism: A Twentieth-Century Perspective*, 2nd edn, revised (Detroit: Wayne State University Press, 1980).

Brodie, T.L., 'Greco-Roman Imitation of Texts as a Partial Guide to Luke's Use of Sources', in: *Luke-Acts: New Perspectives from the Society of Biblical Literature Seminar*, ed. Charles H. Talbert (New York: Crossroad, 1984), pp. 17-46.

Bünker, M., *Briefformular und rhetorische Disposition im 1. Korintherbrief* (Göttingen: Göttinger Theologische Arbeiten, 28; Vandenhoeck und Ruprecht, 1984)

Bultmann, R., *Der Stil der paulinischen Predigt und die kynisch-stoische Diatribe* (FRLANT 13; Göttingen: Vandenhoeck & Ruprecht, 1910; repr. 1984).

Church, F.F., 'Rhetorical Structure and Design in Paul's Letter to Philemon', *HTR* 61 (1978), pp. 17-33.

Cicero. *De inventione, De optimo genere oratorum, Topica*, English translation by H.M. Hubbell (LCL; Cambridge: Harvard University Press, 1949).

Cicero. *De oratore, De fato, Paradoxa stoicorum, De partitione oratoria*, two volumes; English translation by E. W. Sutton and H. Rackham (LCL; Cambridge: Harvard University Press, 1942).

Cicero. *Letters to Atticus*, three volumes; English translation by E.O. Winstedt (LCL; London: William Heinemann, 1912-18).

Cicero. *Letters to his Friends*, three volumes; English translation by W. Glynn Williams (LCL; Cambridge: Harvard University Press, 1958-60).

Clark, D.L., *Rhetoric in Greco-Roman Education* (New York: Columbia University Press, 1957).

Classen, C.J., *Recht—Rhetorik—Politik: Untersuchungen zu Ciceros rhetorischer Strategie* (Darmstadt: Wissenschaftliche Buchgesellschaft, 1985).

Clines, D.J.A., D.M. Gunn, and A.J. Hauser, eds., *Art and Meaning: Rhetoric in Biblical Literature* (JSOTS 19; Sheffield: JSOT Press, 1982).

Davies, W.D., Review of H.D. Betz, *Galatians*, in: *RelSRev* 7 (1981), pp. 310-18; repr. in Davies, *Jewish and Pauline Studies* (Philadelphia: Fortress Press, 1984), pp. 172-88.

Demetrii et Libanii qui feruntur Typoi Epistolikoi et Epistolimaioi Charactēres, ed. V. Weichert (Leipzig: B.G. Teubner, 1910).

Demetrius. *On Style*, English translation by W.R. Roberts (LCL; Cambridge: Harvard University Press, 1927).

Demosthenes. *Funeral Speech, Erotic Essay, Exordia, Letters*, English translation by N.W. and N.J. DeWitt (LCL; Cambridge: Harvard University Press, 1949).

Dobson, J.F., *The Greek Orators* (London: Methuen, 1918; repr. Chicago: Ares Publishers, 1974).

Douglas, A.E., Review of H. Lausberg, *Handbuch der literarischen Rhetorik*, in: *Classical Review* n.s. 12 (1962), pp. 246-47.

Erasmus, *De conscribendis epistolis*, in: *Omnia opera Desiderii Erasmi Roterodami recognita et adnotatione critica instructa notisque illustrata* (Amsterdam: North Holland Publishing Co., 1971), with introduction and notes by J.-C. Margolin, I/2, pp. 153-579.

Forbes, C., 'Comparison, Self-Praise, and Irony: Paul's Boasting and the Conventions of Hellenistic Rhetoric', *NTS* 32 (1986), pp. 1-30.

Goldstein, J.A., *The Letters of Demosthenes* (New York & London: Columbia University Press, 1968).

Grimaldi, W.M.A., S.J., *Aristotle, Rhetoric I: A Commentary* (New York: Fordham University Press, 1980).

Heinrici, C.F.G., *Der zweite Brief an die Korinther, mit einem Anhang: Zum Hellenismus des Paulus* (MeyerK 6; 8th edn; Göttingen: Vandenhoeck & Ruprecht, 1900).

Hellwig, A., *Untersuchungen zur Theorie der Rhetorik bei Platon und Aristoteles* (Hypomnemata, 38; Göttingen: Vandenhoeck & Ruprecht, 1973).

Hinks, D.A.G., 'Tria genera causarum', *Classical Quarterly* 30 (1936), pp. 170-76.

Hübner, H., 'Der Galaterbrief und das Verhältnis von antiker Rhetorik und Epistolographie', *TLZ* 109 (1984), cols. 241-50.

Hughes, F.W., 'New Testament Rhetorical Criticism and its Methodology', paper presented at the Society of Biblical Literature meeting in Atlanta, Georgia, November, 1986.

—'The Rhetoric of the Four-Chapter Letter (2 Corinthians 10-13)', paper presented at the Society of Biblical Literature meeting in Anaheim, California, November, 1985.

Jackson, J.J.; and M. Kessler, eds., *Rhetorical Criticism: Essays in Honor of James Muilenburg* (Pittsburgh: Pickwick Press, 1974).

Jebb, R.C., *The Attic Orators from Antiphon to Isaeos*, two volumes (London: Macmillan, 1876; repr. New York: Russell & Russell, 1962).

Jennrich, W.A., 'Classical Rhetoric in the New Testament', *Classical Journal* 44 (1948-49), pp. 30-32.

Jewett, R., 'The Epistolary Thanksgiving and the Integrity of Philippians', *NovT* 12 (1970), pp. 40-53.

—'Romans as an Ambassadorial Letter', *Int* 36 (1982), pp. 5-20.

Judge, E.A., 'The Early Christians as a Scholastic Community', *Journal of Religious History* 1 (1960), pp. 4-15, 125-37.

—'Paul's Boasting in Relation to Contemporary Professional Practice', *AusBR* 16 (1968), pp. 37-50.

Kennedy, G.A., *The Art of Persuasion in Greece* (A History of Rhetoric, 1; Princeton: Princeton University Press, 1963).

—*The Art of Rhetoric in the Roman World 300 B.C.–A.D. 300* (A History of Rhetoric, 2; Princeton: Princeton University Press, 1972).

—*Classical Rhetoric and its Christian and Secular Tradition from Ancient to Modern Times* (Chapel Hill: University of North Carolina Press, 1980).

—'Focusing of Arguments in Greek Deliberative Oratory', *TAPA* 90 (1959), pp. 131-38.

—*Greek Rhetoric under Christian Emperors* (A History of Rhetoric, 3; Princeton: Princeton University Press, 1983).

—*New Testament Interpretation through Rhetorical Criticism* (Studies in Religion; Chapel Hill: University of North Carolina Press, 1984).

—*Quintilian* (Twayne World Authors Series; New York: Twayne, 1969).

—Review of A.D. Leeman, *Orationis Ratio*, in: *American Journal of Philology* 87 (1963), pp. 237-41.

Knorr, D.E., 'The Rhetorical Consensus: A Proposed Methodology for the Study of Paul's Use of the Old Testament', paper presented at the Midwest regional meeting of the Society of Biblical Literature, Andrews University, February 20, 1986.

Koskenniemi, H., 'Cicero über die Briefarten (genera epistularum)', *Arctos* n.F. 1 (1954), pp. 97-102.

—*Studien zur Idee und Phraseologie des griechischen Briefes bis 400 n. Chr.* (Annales Academiae Scientiarum Fennicae, B 102/2; Helsinki: Suomalaien Tiedakatemie, & Wiesbaden: Otto Harrassowitz, 1956).

Kroll, W., 'Rhetorik', in PWSup (Stuttgart: Metzler, 1940), Vol. VII, cols. 1039-1138.

Kurz, W.S., 'Hellenistic Rhetoric and the Christological Proof of Luke–Acts', *CBQ* 42 (1980), pp. 171-95.

Lausberg, H., *Handbuch der literarischen Rhetorik: Eine Grundlegung der Literaturwissenschaft*, two volumes (2nd edn; Munich: Max Hueber, 1973).

Bibliography 139

Leeman, A.D., *Orationis Ratio: The Stylistic Theories and Practice of the Roman Orators, Historians, and Philosophers*, two volumes (Amsterdam: Adolf M. Hakkert, 1963).

Malherbe, A.J., 'Ancient Epistolary Theorists', *Ohio Journal of Religious Studies* 5 (1977), pp. 3-77.

—*Moral Exhortation, A Greco-Roman Sourcebook* (Library of Early Christianity, 4; Philadelphia: Westminster Press, 1986).

Marrou, H.-I., *A History of Education in Antiquity*, translated by George Lamb (New York: Sheed & Ward, 1956; repr. Madison: University of Wisconsin Press, 1982).

Martin, J., *Antike Rhetorik* (Handbuch der Altertumswissenschaft, II/3; Munich: C.H. Beck, 1974).

Meeks, W.A., Review of H.D. Betz, *Galatians*, in: *JBL* 100 (1981), pp. 304-307.

Muilenburg, J., 'Form Criticism and Beyond', *JBL* 88 (1969), pp. 1-18.

Murphy, J.J., *Medieval Eloquence: Studies in the Theory and Practice of Mediaeval Rhetoric* (Berkeley: University of California Press, 1978).

—*Rhetoric in the Middle Ages: A History of Rhetorical Theory from Saint Augustine to the Renaissance* (Berkeley: University of California Press, 1974).

—*Three Medieval Rhetorical Arts* (Berkeley: University of California Press, 1971).

Neyrey, J., 'The Forensic Defense Speech and Paul's Trial Speeches in Acts 22-26: Form and Function', in: *Luke–Acts: New Perspectives from the Society of Biblical Literature Seminar*, ed. Charles H. Talbert (New York: Crossroad, 1984), pp. 210-24.

Norden, E., *Die antike Kunstprosa vom VI. Jahrhundert vor Christus bis in die Zeit der Renaissance* (Stuttgart: B.G. Teubner, 1913; repr. Darmstadt: Wissenschaftliche Buchgesellschaft, 1958).

Parks, E.P., F.S.C., *The Roman Rhetorical Schools as a Preparation for the Courts Under the Early Empire* (Johns Hopkins University Studies in Historical and Political Science, 63/2; Baltimore: Johns Hopkins Press, 1945).

Pearson, L., *The Art of Demosthenes* (American Philological Association Special Publications, 4; Chico: Scholars Press, 1981).

Patton, J., 'Wisdom and Eloquence: The Alliance of Exegesis and Rhetoric in Augustine', *Central States Speech Journal* 28 (1977), pp. 96-105.

Peter, H., *Der Brief in der römischen Literatur* (Abhandlungen der Königlichen Sächsischen Gesellschaft der Wissenschaften, philologisch-historische Classe, 20/3; Leipzig: B.G. Teubner; repr. Hildesheim: Georg Olms, 1965).

Prill, P., 'Cicero in Theory and Practice: The Securing of Good Will in the *Exordia* of Five Forensic Speeches', *Rhetorica* 4 (1986), pp. 93-109.

[Pseudo-Cicero,] *Rhetorica ad Herennium*, translated by H. Caplan (LCL; Cambridge: Harvard University Press, 1954).

Quintilian, *The Institutio Oratoria of Quintilian*, English translation by H. E. Butler, four volumes (LCL; Cambridge: Harvard University Press, 1920-22).

Rabe, H., 'Aus Rhetoren-Handschriften: 9. Griechische Briefsteller', *Rheinisches Museum für Philologie* n.F. 64 (1909), pp. 284-309.

Rockinger, L., *Über Briefsteller und Formelbücher in Deutschland während des Mittelalters* (München: J.G. Weiss, 1861).

Radermacher, L., *Artium Scriptores: Reste der voraristotelischen Rhetorik* (Sitzungberichte der österreichischen Akademie der Wissenschaften, philosophisch-historische Klasse, 227/3; Wien: Rudolf M. Rohrer, 1951).

Robbins, V.K., Review of George A. Kennedy, *New Testament Interpretation through Rhetorical Criticism*, in: *Rhetorica* 3 (1985), pp. 145-49.

140   *Early Christian Rhetoric and 2 Thessalonians*

Robbins, V.K. & Patton, J.H., 'Rhetoric and Biblical Criticism', *Quarterly Journal of Speech* 66 (1980), pp. 327-50.

Roberts, W.R., *Greek Rhetoric and Literary Criticism* (New York: Longmans, Green & Co., 1928).

Roetzel, C.J., *The Letters of Paul: Conversations in Context*, second edn (Atlanta: John Knox Press, 1982).

Ruether, R.R., *Gregory of Nazianzus: Rhetor and Philosopher* (Oxford: Clarendon Press, 1969).

Sider, R.D., *Ancient Rhetoric and the Art of Tertullian* (Oxford Theological Monographs; Oxford: Oxford University Press, 1971).

Siegert, F., *Argumentation bei Paulus gezeigt an Röm 9-11* (WUNT 34; Tübingen: J.C.B. Mohr [Paul Siebeck], 1985).

Solmsen, F., 'The Aristotelian Tradition in Ancient Rhetoric', *American Journal of Philology* 62 (1941), pp. 35-50, 169-90.

Spencer, A.B., *Paul's Literary Style: A Stylistic and Historical Comparison of II Corinthians 11:16-12:13, Romans 8:9-39, and Philippians 3:2-4:13* (Evangelical Theological Society Monograph Series; Jackson, Miss.: Evangelical Theological Society, 1984).

Spengel, L., ed., *Rhetores Graeci* (Leipzig: B.G.Teubner, 1894).

Stead, G.C., 'Rhetorical Method in Athanasius', *VC* 30 (1976), pp. 127-31.

Stowers, S.K., *The Diatribe and Paul's Letter to the Romans* (SBLDS 57; Chico: Scholars Press, 1981).

—*Letter Writing in Greco-Roman Antiquity* (Library of Early Christianity, 5; Philadelphia: Westminster Press, 1986).

Thraede, K., *Grundzüge griechisch-römischer Brieftopik* (Zetemata, 48; Munich: C.H. Beck, 1970).

Vigna, G.S., 'The Influence of Epideictic Rhetoric on Eusebius of Caesarea's Political Theology' (Ph.D. dissertation, Northwestern University/Garrett-Evangelical Theological Seminary, 1980).

Volkmann, R., *Die Rhetorik der Griechen und Römer in systematischer Übersicht*, 2nd edn (Leipzig: B.G. Teubner, 1885).

Weische, A., *Ciceros Nachahmung der attischen Redner* (Bibliothek der klassischen Altertumswissenschaften, n.F. 2/45; Heidelberg: Winter, 1972).

Weiss, J., 'Beiträge zur Paulinischen Rhetorik', in: *Theologische Studien. Herrn Wirk. Oberkonsistorialrath Professor D. Bernhard Weiss zu seinem 70. Geburtstage dargebracht* (Göttingen: Vandenhoeck & Ruprecht, 1897), pp. 165-247.

White, J.L., *The Form and Function of the Body of the Greek Letter: A Study of the Letter-Body in the Non-Literary Papyri and in Paul the Apostle*, second edn, corrected (SBLDS 2; Missoula: Scholars Press, 1972).

—*Light from Ancient Letters* (Foundations and Facets: New Testament; Philadelphia: Fortress Press, 1986).

—'New Testament Epistolary Literature in the Framework of Ancient Epistolography', *Aufstieg und Niedergang der römischen Welt*, ed. Wolfgang Haas (Berlin & New York: Walter de Gruyter, 1984), II.25.2, pp. 1730-56.

—'Saint Paul and the Apostolic Letter Tradition', *CBQ* 45 (1983), pp. 433-44.

Wilder, A.N., *The Language of the Gospel: Early Christian Rhetoric* (New York: Harper & Row, 1964).

Wilke, C.G., *Die neutestamentliche Rhetorik: Ein Seitenstück zur Grammatik des neutestamentlichen Sprachidioms* (Leipzig: Arnold, 1843).

Wooten, C.W., *Cicero's Philippics and their Demosthenic Model: The Rhetoric of Crisis* (Chapel Hill: University of North Carolina Press, 1983).

Wuellner, W., 'Greek Rhetoric and Pauline Argumentation', in: *Early Christian Literature and the Classical Intellectual Tradition: In honorem Robert M. Grant*, ed. W.R. Schoedel & R.L. Wilken (Théologie historique, 53; Paris: Éditions Beauchesne, 1979), pp. 177-88.

—'Paul's Rhetoric of Argumentation in Romans: An Alternative to the Donfried-Karris Debate Over Romans', *CBQ* 38 (1976), pp. 330-51; repr. in: *The Romans Debate*, ed. K.P. Donfried (Minneapolis: Augsburg Publishing House, 1977), pp. 152-74.

—'Where is Rhetorical Criticism Taking Us?' *CBQ* 49 (1987), pp. 448-63.

Other Works

Achtemeier, P.J., 'An Apocalyptic Shift in Early Christian Tradition: Reflections on Some Canonical Evidence', *CBQ* 45 (1983), pp. 231-48.

Aland, K., 'The Problem of Anonymity and Pseudonymity in Christian Literature of the First Two Centuries', *JTS* n.s. 12 (1961), pp. 39-49.

Aleith, E., *Paulusverständnis in der alten Kirche* (BZNW 18; Berlin: Alfred Töpelmann, 1937).

Aune, D.E., *The Cultic Setting of Realized Eschatology in Early Christianity* (NovTSup 28; Leiden: E.J. Brill, 1972).

Barnett, A.E., *Paul Becomes a Literary Influence* (Chicago: University of Chicago Press, 1941).

Barrett, C.K., 'Pauline Controversies in the Post-Pauline Period', *NTS* 20 (1973-74), pp. 229-45.

Barth, M., *Ephesians*, two volumes (AB 38-38a; Garden City: Doubleday, 1974).

Bauer, W., *A Greek-English Lexicon of the New Testament and Other Early Christian Literature*, translated and adapted from the German by W.F. Arndt and F.W. Gingrich, second edn revised and augmented by F.W. Gingrich and F.W. Danker (Chicago: University of Chicago Press, 1979).

Beker, J.C., *Paul the Apostle: The Triumph of God in Life and Thought* (Philadelphia: Fortress Press, 1980).

Betz, H.D., 'Gottmensch II (Griechisch-römische Antike und Urchristentum)', in: *RAC*, ed. Theodor Klauser (Stuttgart: Anton Hiersemann, 1983), Vol. XII, cols. 234-312.

de Boer, M.C., 'Images of Paul in the Post-Apostolic Period', *CBQ* 42 (1980), pp. 363-64.

Bousset, W., *Der Antichrist in der Überlieferung des Judentums, des Neuen Testaments und der alten Kirche. Ein Beitrag zur Auslegung der Apocalypse* (Göttingen: Vandenhoeck & Ruprecht, 1895).

Brox, N., *Falsche Verfasserangaben: Zur Erklärung der frühchristlichen Pseudepigraphie* (SBS 79; Stuttgart: Katholisches Bibelwerk, 1975).

—*Die Pastoralbriefe* (RNT 7/2, 4th edn; Regensburg: Friedrich Pustet, 1969.

—ed., *Pseudepigraphie in der heidnischen und jüdisch-christlichen Antike* (Wege der Forschung, 484; Darmstadt: Wissenschaftliche Buchgesellschaft, 1977).

—'Zum Problemstand in der Erforschung der altchristlichen Pseudepigraphie', *Kairos* 15 (1973), pp. 10-23.

Buck, C.; and Taylor, G., *Saint Paul: A Study in the Development of his Thought* (New York: Charles Scribner, 1969).

Campenhausen, H. von, *Ecclesiastical Authority and Spiritual Power in the Church of the First Three Centuries*, translated by J.A. Baker (Stanford: Stanford University Press, 1969).

Collins, A.Y., *Crisis and Catharsis: The Power of the Apocalypse* (Philadelphia: Westminster Press, 1984).

Collins, J.J., *The Apocalyptic Imagination: An Introduction to the Jewish Matrix of Christianity* (New York: Crossroad, 1984) .

—ed., *Apocalypse: The Morphology of a Genre* (*Semeia* 14; Missoula: Scholars Press, 1979).

Collins, R.F., 'The Image of Paul in the Pastorals', *Laval théologique et philosophique* 31 (1975), pp. 147-73.

Cullmann, O., 'Wann kommt das Reich Gottes? Zur Enderwartung der Christlichen Schriftsteller des zweiten Jahrhunderts', in: *Vorträge und Aufsätze 1925-1962*, ed. K. Fröhlich (Tübingen: J.C.B. Mohr [Paul Siebeck], 1967), pp. 535-47.

Dassmann, E., *Der Stachel im Fleisch: Paulus in der frühchristlichen Literatur bis Irenäus* (Münster: Aschendorff, 1979).

Deissmann, A., *Light from the Ancient East: The New Testament Illustrated by Recently Discovered Texts of the Graeco-Roman World* , 4th edn, translated by L.R.M. Strachan (London: Hodder & Stoughton, 1911; repr. Grand Rapids: Baker Book House, 1978).

Dibelius, M. & Conzelmann, H., *The Pastoral Epistles: A Commentary on the Pastoral Epistles*, translated by P. Butolph and A. Yarbro, ed. H. Koester (Hermeneia: Philadelphia: Fortress Press, 1972).

Donelson, L.R., *Pseudepigraphy and Ethical Argument in the Pastoral Epistles* (Hermeneutische Untersuchung zur Theologie, 22; Tübingen: J.C.B. Mohr [Paul Siebeck], 1986).

Doty, W.G., *Letters in Primitive Christianity* (Guides to Biblical Scholarship; Philadelphia: Fortress Press, 1973).

Fenton, J.C., 'Pseudonymity in the New Testament', *Theology* 58 (1955), pp. 51-56.

Fiorenza, E.S., *In Memory of Her: A Feminist Theological Reconstruction of Christian Origins* (New York: Crossroad, 1983).

Fischer, K.M., *Tendenz und Absicht des Epheserbriefes* (FRLANT 111; Göttingen: Vandenhoeck & Ruprecht, 1973).

Fossum, J., 'Jewish Christian Christology and Jewish Mysticism', *VC* 37 (1983), pp. 260-87.

Francis, F.O., 'The Christological Argument of Colossians', in: *God's Christ and his People: Studies in Honour of Nils Alstrup Dahl*, ed. J. Jervell & W.A. Meeks (Oslo: Universitetsforlaget, 1977), pp. 192-208.

Funk, R.W., 'The Apostolic Parousia: Form and Significance', in: *Christian History and Interpretation: Studies Presented to John Knox*, ed. W.R. Farmer, C.F.D. Moule, and R.R. Niebuhr (Cambridge: Cambridge University Press, 1967), pp. 249-68.

Furnish, V.P. *II Corinthians* (AB 32A; Garden City: Doubleday, 1984).

Gnilka, J., 'Das Paulusbild im Kolosser- und Epheserbrief', in: *Kontinuität und Einheit: Für Franz Mussner*, ed. P.-G. Mller & W. Stenger (Freiburg, Basel, Vienna: Herder, 1981), pp. 179-93.

—*Der Kolosserbrief* (HTKNT X/1; Freiburg, Basel, Vienna: Herder, 1980).

—*Der Epheserbrief* (HTKNT X/2; Freiburg, Basel, Vienna: Herder, 1971).

Goldstein, J.A., *I Maccabees: A New Translation with Introduction and Commentary* (AB 41; Garden City: Doubleday & Co., 1976).

Goodspeed, E.J., *The Meaning of Ephesians* (Chicago: University of Chicago Press, 1933).

Groh, D.E., 'Crisis in the Household: Affection and Defection in Early Christianity', Presidential Address, Second Independent Conference of the North American Patristic Society (NAPS), given May 20, 1983, at Loyola University of Chicago.

Harrington, D.J., S.J., *Light of All Nations: Essays on the Church in New Testament Research* (Good News Studies, 3; Wilmington: Michael Glazier, 1982).

Harris, H., *The Tübingen School* (Oxford: Clarendon Press, 1975).

Hendrix, H.L., 'Thessalonicans Honor Romans' (Th.D. dissertation, Harvard University, 1984).

Hicks, E.L., 'St. Paul and Hellenism', *Studia Biblica et Ecclesiastica* 4 (1896), pp. 1-14.

Hughes, F.W., 'Feminism and Early Christian History, *ATR* 69 (1987), pp. 287-99.

Jewett, R., *A Chronology of Paul's Life* (Philadelphia: Fortress Press, 1979).

Jülicher, A., *An Introduction to the New Testament*, translated by Janet Penrose Ward (London: Smith, Elder, & Co., 1904).

Käsemann, E., *Leib und Leib Christi: Eine Untersuchung zur paulinischen Begrifflichkeit* (BHT 9; Tübingen: J.C.B. Mohr [Paul Siebeck], 1933).

—*Das Neue Testament als Kanon* (Göttingen: Vandenhoeck & Ruprecht, 1970).

—*New Testament Questions of Today* (Philadelphia: Fortress Press, 1969).

Keck, L.E., 'Paul and Apocalyptic Theology', *Int* 38 (1984), pp. 229-41.

Kiley, M., *Colossians as Pseudepigraphy* (Biblical Seminar, 4; Sheffield: JSOT Press, 1986).

Koester, H., *History and Literature of Early Christianity*, Vol. II of *Introduction to the New Testament* (Foundations and Facets: New Testament; Philadelphia: Fortress; Berlin & New York, Walter de Gruyter, 1982).

Lindemann, A., *Die Aufhebung der Zeit: Geschichtsverständnis und Eschatologie im Epheserbrief* (SNT 12; Gütersloh: Gerd Mohn, 1975).

—*Der Kolosserbrief* (Zürcher Bibelkommentare: Neues Testament, 10; Zürich: Theologischer Verlag, 1983).

—*Der Epheserbrief* (Zürcher Bibelkommentare: Neues Testament, 8; Zürich: Theologischer Verlag, 1985).

—*Paulus im ältesten Christentum: Das Bild des Apostels und die Rezeption der paulinischen Theologie in der frühchristlichen Literatur bis Marcion* (BHT 58; Tübingen: J.C.B. Mohr [Paul Siebeck], 1979).

Lohse, E., 'Christusherrschaft und Kirche im Kolosserbrief', *NTS* 11 (1964-65), pp. 203-16.

—*Colossians and Philemon: A Commentary on the Epistles to the Colossians and to Philemon* (Hermeneia; Philadelphia: Fortress Press, 1971).

—*The Formation of the New Testament*, translated by M. Eugene Boring (Nashville: Abingdon Press, 1981).

Ludwig, H., 'Der Verfasser des Kolosserbriefes—Ein Schüler des Paulus' (Dr.theol. dissertation, Georg-August-Universität Göttingen, 1974).

MacDonald, D.R., *The Legend and the Apostle: The Battle for Paul in Story and Canon* (Philadelphia: Westminster Press, 1983).

Marxsen, W., *Introduction to the New Testament: An Approach to Its Problems*, translated by G. Buswell (Oxford: Basil Blackwell, 1968).

Meade, D.G., *Pseudonymity and Canon: An Investigation into the Relationship of Authorship and Authority in Jewish and Earliest Christian Tradition* (WUNT 39; J.C.B. Mohr [Paul Siebeck], 1986).

Meeks, W.A., 'In One Body: The Unity of Humankind in Colossians and Ephesians',

144   *Early Christian Rhetoric and 2 Thessalonians*

in: *God's Christ and his People: Studies in Honour of Nils Alstrup Dahl*, ed. J. Jervell & W.A. Meeks (Oslo: Universitetsforlaget, 1977), pp. 209-21.

—*The First Urban Christians: The Social World of the Apostle Paul* (New Haven: Yale University Press, 1983).

Merklein, H., 'Eph 4,1-5,20 als Rezeption von Kol 3,1-17 (zugleich ein Beitrag zur Pragmatik des Epheserbriefen', in: *Kontinuität und Einheit: Für Franz Mussner*, ed. P.-G. Müller & W. Stenger (Freiburg: Herder, 1981), pp. 194-210.

—'Paulinische Theologie in der Rezeption des Kolosser- und Epheserbriefes', in: *Paulus in den neutestamentlichen Spätschriften: Zur Paulusrezeption im Neuen Testament*, ed. K. Kertelge (Quaestiones disputatae, 89; Freiburg, Basel, Wien: Herder, 1981), pp. 25-69.

—*Das kirchliche Amt nach dem Epheserbrief* (SANT; München: Kösel, 1973).

Metzger, B.M., 'Literary Forgeries and Canonical Pseudepigrapha', *JBL* 91 (1972), pp. 1-24.

Mitton, C.L., *The Epistle to the Ephesians: Its Authorship, Origin and Purpose* (Oxford: Oxford University Press, 1951).

—*The Formation of the Pauline Corpus of Letters* (London: Epworth, 1955).

Mørkholm, O., *Antiochus IV of Syria* (Classica et mediaevalia, dissertationes, 8; Copenhagen: Gyldendal, 1966).

Mussner, F., *Der Brief an die Epheser* (Ökumenischer Taschenbuchkommentar zum Neuen Testament, 10; Gütersloh, Gerd Mohn, and Würzburg: Echter-Verlag, 1982).

—*Christus das All und die Kirche: Studien zur Theologie des Epheserbriefes* (Trierer theologische Studien, 5; Trier: Paulinus, 1955).

Nielsen, C.M., 'The Status of Paul and his Letters in Colossians', *Perspectives in Religious Studies* 12 (1985), pp. 103-22.

Percy, E., *Die Probleme der Kolosser- und Epheserbriefe* (Skrifter utg. av Kung. Humanistiska vetenskapssamfundet i Lund, 39; Lund: C.W.K. Gleerup, 1946).

Pfleiderer, O., *Paulinism: A Contribution to the History of Primitive Christian Theology*, translated by E. Peters, two volumes (London: Williams & Norgate, 1891).

Pobee, J.S., *Persecution and Martyrdom in the Theology of Paul* (JSNTS 6; Sheffield: JSOT Press, 1985).

Pokorny, P., *Der Brief des Paulus an die Kolosser* (Theologischer Handkommentar zum Neuen Testament, X/1; Berlin: Evangelische Verlagsanstalt, 1987).

Rensberger, D.K., 'As the Apostle Teaches: The Development of the Use of Paul's Letters in Second-Century Christianity' (Ph.D. dissertation, Yale University, 1981).

Rigaux, B., O.F.M., *L'Antichrist, et l'opposition au royaume messianique dans l'Ancien et le Nouveau Testament* (Gembloux: J. Duculot, 1932).

Roon, A. van, *The Authenticity of Ephesians* (NovTSup 39; Leiden: E.J. Brill, 1974).

Rudolph, K., *Gnosis: The Nature and History of Gnosticism*, translation ed. R.McL. Wilson (San Francisco: Harper & Row, 1983).

—'Urmensch', in: *RGG*, third edn (Tübingen: J.C.B. Mohr [Paul Siebeck], 1962), Vol. VI, cols. 1195-97.

Schade, H.-H., *Apokalyptische Christologie bei Paulus: Studien zum Zussamenhang von Christologie und Eschatologie in den Paulusbriefen* (Göttinger Theologische Arbeiten, 18; Göttingen: Vandenhoeck & Ruprecht, 1981).

Schenke, H.-M., 'Der Wiederstreit gnostischer und kirchlicher Christologie im Spiegel des, Kolosserbriefes, *ZTK* 61 (1964), pp. 391-403.

Schenke, H.-M., & K.M. Fischer, *Die Briefe des Paulus und Schriften des Paulinismus*, Vol. I of *Einleitung in die Schriften des Neuen Testaments* (Gütersloh: Gerd Mohn, 1978).

Schille, G., *Das älteste Paulus-Bild: Beobachtungen zur lukanischen und zur deutero-paulinischen Paulus-Darstellung* (Berlin: Evangelische Verlagsanstalt, 1979).

Schlier, H., *Christus und die Kirche im Epheserbrief* (BHT 6; Tübingen: J.C.B. Mohr [Paul Siebeck], 1930).

Schnackenburg, R., *Der Brief an die Epheser* (EKKNT X; Zürich, Einsiedeln, Cologne: Benziger Verlag; Neukirchen-Vluyn: Neukirchener Verlag, 1982).

Schoedel, W.R., *Ignatius of Antioch: A Commentary on the Letters of Ignatius of Antioch* (Hermeneia; Philadelphia: Fortress Press, 1985).

Schubert, P., *Form and Function of the Pauline Thanksgivings* (BZNW 20; Berlin: Alfred Töpelmann, 1939).

Schweizer, E., *The Letter to the Colossians*, translated by Andrew Chester (Minneapolis: Augsburg Publishing House, 1982).

—'The Letter to the Colossians—Neither Pauline nor Post-Pauline?' in: *Pluralisme et oecuménisme en recherches théologiques: Mélanges offerts au R.P. Dockx*, ed. Y. Congar, G. Dejaijve, H. de Lubac (Paris and Louvain: Gembloux, 1976), pp. 3-16.

Smyth, H.W., *Greek Grammar*, revised by G.M. Messing (Cambridge: Harvard University Press, 1956).

Speyer, W., *Die literarische Fälschung im heidnischen und christlichen Altertum: Ein Versuch ihrer Deutung* (Handbuch der Altertumswissenschaft, I/2; Munich: C.H. Beck, 1971).

Spicq, C., O.P., *Les Épîtres Pastorales*, 4th edn (EBib; Paris: J. Gabalda, 1969).

Staerk, W., *Die Erlöserwartung in den östlichen Religionen: Untersuchungen zu den Ausdrucksformen der biblischen Christologie (Soter II)* (Stuttgart & Berlin: W. Kohlhammer, 1938.

Towner, P.H., 'The Present Age in the Eschatology of the Pastoral Epistles', *NTS* 32 (1986), pp. 427-48.

Vacalopoulos, A.E., *A History of Thessaloniki*, English translation by T.F. Carney (Thessaloniki: Institute for Balkan Studies, 1963).

Vielhauer, P., *Geschichte der urchristlichen Literatur: Einleitung in das Neue Testament, die Apokryphen und die Apostolischen Väter* (Berlin & New York: Walter de Gruyter, 1975; repr. 1978).

Weiss, J., *Earliest Christianity: A History of the Period A.D. 30-150*, English translation ed. F.C. Grant (Harper Torchbooks; New York: Harper, 1959).

Welles, C.B., ed., *Royal Correspondence in the Hellenistic Period: A Study in Greek Epigraphy* (New Haven: Yale University Press, 1934).

INDEX

INDEX OF BIBLICAL REFERENCES

Joshua
22.22   58

2 Chronicles
28.19   58
33.19   58

Job
4.9 LXX   119n26

Psalms
32.6 LXX   119n26
88.23 LXX   128n

Isaiah
11.4 LXX   60, 128n18
53.3 LXX   128n18
66 LXX   60
66.6 LXX   60

Jeremiah
2.19   58

Daniel
11.36   128n18

1 Maccabees
2.15   58

Matthew
24.3-8   58
24.4-36   121n12
24.23-28   119n28

Mark
13.3-37   121n12
13.21-23   119n28

Luke
21.8-36   121n12

Romans
1.7b   117n3
5.3-5   20
8.20   119n31
8.23   119n30
11.16   119n30
16.4   67
16.5   63, 119n30
16.17-20   98

1 Corinthians
1.2   117n3
3.6ff.   61
6.9   58
13   21, 23
15.20   119n30
15.23   119n30
15.33   58
16.15   119n30

2 Corinthians
1.7   63
8-9   23
10.10   19, 29, 67
11.6   22
11.16-30   20

Galatians
1.3   117n3
5.1-6.10   63
6.7   118n17

Ephesians
1.2   117n3
1.3   90
1.7   90
1.10   90
1.13-14   90
1.20   90
1.21-22   90

2.6   90
2.14-16   90
2.15   90
2.21-22   90
2.22   94
3.1-6   126n51
3.2   90, 100
3.3   90
3.8   91, 126n51
3.10   91
3.13   125n48
3.14-16   126n51
3.14   14, 66, 78, 82
4.1-16   14, 94
4.1   119n31
4.4-6   94
4.20-21   126n51
4.22-24   91
5.17-20   94
6.10-17   94
6.18   94

Philippians
1.2   117n3

Colossians
1.5-7   126n51
1.8   88, 126n54
1.10   119n31
1.11-14   123n28
1.15-20   87, 100
1.16-18   124n32
1.19   87
1.23   100
1.24-26   124n35
1.24   87, 123n29
1.25   90
1.27-28   88
1.27   90

Colossians (cont.)		*2 Thessalonians*			101-102
2.5	87, 93, 125n48	1.1-12	51-56	2.12	14, 76
2.8	118n17	1.1-2	51	2.13-15	57, 61, 77
2.9	87	1.1	92	2.13	57
2.14-15	14	1.2	52	2.14	14
2.14	88	1.3-5	53	2.15	14, 57, 76-78, 92, 94, 102
2.15	88	1.3-4	53		
2.16	124n36	1.3	92	2.16-17	62-63
2.20-21	124n36	1.4-5	54	2.16	62, 92, 102
2.20-23	100	1.4	53-54, 82	2.17	62, 92
3.4	123n26	1.5-9	76	3	65
3.5	124n37	1.5-7	14	3.1-15	55, 63-66
3.9-11	124n37	1.5	53-54, 64	3.1-4	64
3.9	90	1.6-10	54	3.1	64
3.16	93	1.6	53, 92, 102	3.2-3	64
4.7-8	126n51	1.6-7	54	3.2	14, 64, 76, 82, 92-93, 102
4.16	27, 126n51	1.7-10	53		
		1.7	102	3.3	64, 82
1 Timothy		1.8-9	14	3.5	64
1.2	117n3	1.8	53, 55, 76, 92	3.6-15	65
4.1-3	118n17			3.6-13	82, 102
6.14	60	1.9	55	3.6-10	76
6.20	101	1.10	14, 54-55, 92	3.6	65
		1.11-12	55, 92	3.6-7	92
2 Timothy		1.11	55	3.7-9	65
1.10	60	1.12	55-56	3.8	65
4.1	60	2.1-12	84	3.9	65
4.8	60	2.1-2	56-57, 85, 94	3.10-11	65
		2.2-3	92-93	3.10	82, 92, 102
Titus		2.2	14, 16-17, 57, 6, 75-77, 85, 91, 100, 102	3.11	65
1.10	118n17			3.12-15	65
2.13	60			3.13	65. 82, 102
		2.3-17	92	3.14-15	66, 76
1 Thessalonians		2.3-15	57-61	3.14	14, 66, 78, 82, 92, 102
1.1	52	2.3-12	57-58, 62, 77, 82		
1.3	54	2.3	102, 128n18	3.15	82, 102
1.9-10	81	2.3a	58	3.16-18	66-67
2.12	119n31	2.3b-4	58-59	3.16	76, 92
4.7	119n31	2.4	59, 128n18	3.17	14-15, 66-67, 75-79, 92
4.13	110n53	2.5	59, 82, 92		
4.15-17	81, 84	2.6-7	59-60	3.18	67
5.2	81-82	2.8-12	60		
5.3	81	2.8	128n18	*Philemon*	
5.13-14	82	2.9-12	92	3	117n3
5.14	65	2.9	59		
5.19-20	57	2.11-12	77	*James*	
5.19	93	2.11	14, 58, 61,	1.18	119n30
5.27	27				

2 Peter
3   118n22

Revelation
4.1   121n12
13.13-14   119n27
13.13   61
14.4   119n30
19.15   60
19.20   60
22.6   122n12

Acts of Paul and Thekla 101

Alberic of Monte Cassino, *Dictaminum radii*
3.5-6   28
3.6   111n72

Apocalypse of Peter   118n22

Apollonius of Tyana, *Epistle* 19   111n64

Aristotle, *Ars rhetorica*
1.2.1   110n48, 112n91
1.2.3-4   117n2
1.3.3   111n67, 112n84, 116n203, 119n38
1.3.4   112n85, 114nn126,127
1.3.5   115n189
1.6.1   112n86
1.8.7   112n86
1.10.1   111n68
3.12.2   111n62
3.13.3   113n94
3.13.4   32, 40, 115nn157,167
3.14.1   113n105
3.14.2   113n106
3.14.6   113n107
3.14.7   113nn109,110
3.14.11   113nn111,113
3.14.12   113n112
3.16   36
3.16.1   114n120
3.16.6   114n121
3.16.8   114n122
3.16.10   114nn123, 124
3.16.16   114n125
3.17-3-3.18.7 40
3.17.3   115n158

3.17.4   115n159, 117nn10,11
3.17.5   40, 115n160
3.19.1   115nn168-70, 119n34
3.19.4   115n171

Ascension of Isaiah
2.4   58
2.5   58

Augustine, *De doctrina Christiana*
4   19
4.12   107n5, 107n6
4.15   107n8

Boethius, *De topicis differentiis*
1208C   113n102

Cicero, *De inventione*
1.1-5   107n7
1.19   113n95
1.20-21   113n115
1.20   35, 113n114, 114n119
1.22   117nn5,13
1.26   114n116
1.27   37, 38, 114n128
1.28   114nn129,130
1.29   114nn131,132
1.30   114nn133,134
1.31-34   38
1.31-33   56, 117n14
1.31   114nn143-45, 120n2
1.32-33   39
1.32   39, 40, 114nn146,147
1.33   114n148
1.34   115n161
1.78   115n162

Cicero, *De inventione (cont.)*
1.98   115nn172,173
1.100   115nn174,175
1.107-109   115n176
1.109   115n186
2.12   115n190
2.156   115n190

Cicero, *De oratore*
1.86-87   112n79
1.105   112n79
2.33   107n7
2.49   111n65
3.125   107n7
3.142-143   107n7

Cicero, *De partitione oratoria*
27   113n96

Cicero, *Eighth Philippic*
29   119n32

Cicero, *First Philippic*
38   119n32

Cicero, *Pro Publio Quinctio*
96   119n32

Cicero, *Pro Roscio Amerino*
153   119n32

Cicero, *Pro Roscio Comoedo*
50   119n32

Cicero, *Second Philippic*
119   119n32

Cicero, *Seventh Philippic*
25   119n32

Cicero, *Thirteenth Philippic*
6-7   119n33

'Demetrius', *De elocutione*
223-235   109n43
223   24

Demosthenes,
De corona   46, 112n87
324   119n32

Demosthenes, *Epistle* 1   47-50, 55, 63,
                             73
1.3   106n1

Demosthenes, *Second Philippic*
37   119n32

Demosthenes, *Third Philippic*
63-69   46, 47
76   119n32

Didache
16.4   119n27

Dionysius of Halicarnassus, *Isocrates*
2-3   111n63
11-20   111n63

*Epistolimaioi
Charakteres*   25

Erasmus, *De conscribendi epistolis*
28   112n77

Homer, *Odyssey*
7.327   113n111

Isocrates, *De pace*
18-21   45

Isocrates, *Epistle* 1
2   106n2

Isocrates, *Panegyricus*   45

Isocrates, *To Philip*
25-26   106n3

Plato, *Epistle* 13   120n41

Plato, *Menexenus*
246B-249E   119n38

Plutarch, *Life of Demosthenes*
5.5   116n193

Quintilian, *Institutio oratoria*
2.1.1-6   112n80
3.4.9   119n38
3.8-6   113n98

Institutio oratoria (cont.)

3.8.11	113n100
3.8-12	113n99
3.9.1	113n97
4.Pr.6	33
4.1	33, 36
4.1.1	114n117
4.1.5	114nn118, 119
4.2	33, 37
4.2.4	114n135
4.2.5	114n136
4.2.25-28	114n137
4.2.31-32	114n138
4.2.31	38
4.2.36-60	114n139
4.4	33, 39
4.5	33, 39, 56, 117n14
4.5.1	114n149
4.5.22-23	114n151
4.5.22	114n150
4.5.26	115n152
4.5.27	115n153
5	33, 41
5.Pr.5	115n163
6.1	33
6.1.1	115nn177-79
6.1.9	115n180
6.1.11	115n181
9.4.19	111n64

Rationes dictandi

4	28

Rhetorica ad Alexandrum

1421b7	111n203
1421b9	111n69
1421b17-1425b35	119n38
1425b35	111n203

Rhetorica ad Herennium

1.2.2	119n38
1.4	113n101, 115n166
1.6	114n119
1.7	114n119
1.12	38
1.14-16	38
1.14	114n140
1.16	114n141
1.17	115nn154-156
1.18	115n164
2.47	115nn182-84
2.50	115nn185, 187
3.8	41, 115n165

Suetonius, *De grammaticis et rhetoribus*

4	112n80

Thucydides, *History*

2.35	31
2.44.46	119n38

Typoi Epistolikoi   25, 27

INDEX OF MODERN AUTHORS

Achtemeier, P.J. 123n25, 141
Aland, K. 128n9, 132, 141
Aleith, E. 127n2, 141
Alers, G.A. 132
Allo, E.B. 136
Andriessen, P. 132
Askwith, E.H. 132
Aune, D.E. 124n38, 141
Aus, R.D. 60, 119n25, 132

Bahnsen, W. 132
Bailey, J.A. 133
Barnett, A.E. 127n2, 141
Barnouin, M. 133
Barrett, C.K. 127n2, 129n25, 141
Barth, M. 125n42, 141
Bassler, J.M. 117n9, 133
Bauer, W. 118n18, 141
Baur, F.C. 15, 78, 84, 105n4, 133
Beck, I. 113n92, 117n12, 136
Beker, J.C. 86, 123nn23, 24, 141
Berger, K. 23, 109n39, 112n83, 136
Best, E. 106n11, 121n8, 131
Betz, H.D. 22-23, 63, 107n23,
        108nn32,34,36, 118n20,
        119nn35,37, 136, 141
Betz, O. 133
de Boer, M.C. 128n20, 141
Bornemann, W. 121n4, 131
Bousset, W. 141
Braun, H. 133
Brock, B.L. 136
Brodie, T.L. 136
Brox, N. 122n20, 127nn7,9, 141
Bruce, F.F. 106n11, 120n3, 126n52,
        131
Buck, C. 121n5, 141
Bünker, M. 23, 108n37, 137
Bultmann, R. 22, 107n25, 137
Burkeen, W.H. 133

Cadbury, H.J. 7
Campenhausen, H. von 127n7, 141

Church, F.F. 137
Clark, D.L. 137
Classen, C.J. 137
Clemen, C. 133
Clines, D.J.A. 137
Collins, A.Y. 118n23, 142
Collins, J.J. 118n23, 142
Collins, R.F. 128n17, 142
Conzelmann, H. 122n20, 127n7, 142
Coppens, J. 60
Cullmann, O. 60, 119n24, 133

Dassmann, E. 128n23, 142
Dautzenberg, G. 133
Davies, W.D. 108n34, 137
Day, P. 133
Deissmann, A. 142
Dewailly, L.-M. 133
Dibelius, M. 106n10, 122n20, 127n7,
        131, 142
Dobschütz, E. von 131
Dobson, J.F. 111n63, 112n87, 137
Donelson, L.R. 128n9, 142
Donfried, K.P. 133
Doty, W.G. 117n4, 142
Douglas, A.E. 113n103, 133

Eckart, K.-G. 133
Ellicott, C.J. 131
Evans, R.M. 133

Fenton, J.C. 142
Findlay, G.G. 133
Fiorenza, E.S. 101, 128nn14,15,16, 142
Fischer, K.M. 124n31, 125n48, 126n57,
        128n11, 142, 145
Forbes, C. 137
Fossum, J. 142
Frame, J.E. 105n3, 117n16, 126n52,
        131
Francis, F.O. 127n58, 142
Freese, J.H. 113nn93, 108
Friedrich, G. 131

Funk, R.W. 120n40, 142
Furnish, V.P. 106n4, 142

Giblin, C.H. 60
Gnilka, J. 124n38, 126n54, 128n11, 142
Goguel, M. 106n10, 133
Goldstein, J.A. 46-47, 116nn198,202, 118n21, 136, 142
Goodspeed, E.J. 89, 125n40, 142
Graafen, J. 133
Grayston, K. 131
Gregson, R. 121n5, 133
Grimaldi, W.M.A. 43, 115n188, 137
Grimm, C.L.W. 134
Groh, D.E. 120n39, 128n10, 143
Grotius, H. 15, 75, 83, 105n1, 131
Gruner, S. 134
Gunn, D.M. 137

Hadorn, W. 134
Hanson, A.T. 122n20
Harnack, A. von 106n10, 134
Harrington, D.J. 125n44, 143
Harris, H. 143
Hauser, A.J. 137
Heinrici, C.F.G. 21-22, 107nn23,24, 137
Hellwig, A. 112n92, 137
Hendrix, H.L. 143
Hicks, E.L. 143
Hilgenfeld, A. 105n3, 134
Hinks, D.A.G. 112n92, 137
Holland, G.S. 117n8, 117n15, 134
Hollmann, G. 134
Holsten, C. 134
Holtzmann, H.J. 83, 122n16, 134
Hübner, H. 138
Hughes, F.W. 105n1, 134, 109n40, 120n1, 128n14, 134, 138, 143
Hurd, J.C. 78, 121n5, 134

Jackson, J.J. 138
Jebb, R.C. 138
Jennrich, W.A. 108n26, 138
Jewett, R. 22-23, 80-81, 83, 108n35, 109n40, 117nn7,15, 120n41, 121nn7,9,10,11, 122n15, 124n33, 134, 138, 143
Johanson, B.C. 120n41, 134
Jordan, M.D. 119n38

Judge, E.A. 22, 108nn27-31, 138
Jülicher, A. 143

Käsemann, E. 85, 89, 123n22, 124n33, 125n44, 129n23, 143
Kemmler, D.W. 134
Keck, L.E. 123n24, 143
Kennedy, G.A. 8, 22-23, 44, 46-47, 63, 106n3, 108n34, 111nn62,63, 112nn87,88, 113n92, 115n191, 16nn192,194-96,199,120, 119n36, 138
Kern, F.H. 105n3, 134
Kessler, M. 138
Kiley, M. 123nn21,27, 124n34, 143
Knorr, D.E. 109n40, 113n104, 138
Knox, J. 134
Koester, H. 122n21, 123n25, 124n38, 134, 143
Koskenniemi, H. 24, 109n44, 110n47, 138
Krentz, E. 134-35
Krodel, G. 131
Kroll, W. 138
Kurz, W.S. 134

Lake, K. 135
Lausberg, H. 113n103, 138
Leeman, A.D. 111n62, 139
Lightfoot, J.B. 118n16, 131, 135
Lindemann, A. 91, 97-99, 122n21, 125n39, 126nn49,50, 127nn1-6, 135, 143
Lipsius, R.A. 105n3, 135
Lohse, E. 122n21, 124n31, 127n8, 143
Ludwig, H. 123n30, 143
Lünemann, G. 131

MacDonald, D.R. 100-101, 122n20, 128nn13,14, 143
Malherbe, A.J. 24, 109nn41-43, 110nn45-47,52, 119n38, 135, 139
Manson, T.W. 121n5, 135
Marrou, H.-I. 139
Marshall, I.H. 106n11, 120n3, 122n14, 126n52, 131
Martin, J. 117n1, 139
Marxsen, W. 16, 84-85, 106n13, 121n6, 122n19, 131-32, 143
Masson, C. 132

Meade, D.G. 129n24, 143
Meeks, W.A. 107n4, 108n34, 139, 143-44
Merklein, H. 125n39, 126n57, 144
Metzger, B.M. 128n9, 144
Michaelis, W. 135
Milligan, G. 132, 135
Mitton, C.L. 89, 125nn39,41, 144
Morkholm, O. 118n21, 144
Muilenburg, J. 112n83, 139
Murphy, J.J. 28, 111nn70-75, 139
Mussner, F. 144

Neil, W. 131
Neyrey, J. 139
Nielsen, C.M. 128n12, 144
Norden, E. 21, 107nn20-22, 139

Olbrechts-Tyteca, L. 109n38
Orchard, J.B. 135

Parks, E.P. 112n78, 139
Patton, J.H. 109n40, 139-40
Pearson, L. 112n87, 139
Percy, E. 89, 125n43
Perelman, C. 23, 109n38
Peter, H. 26, 111nn59-61, 139
Peterson, R.J. 135
Pfleiderer, O. 127n2, 128n21, 144
Plummer, A. 132
Pobee, J.S. 118n21, 144
Pokorny, P. 144
Prill, P. 114n116, 139

Rabe, H. 111n76, 112n81, 139
Radermacher, L. 113n92, 139
Ramsey, W.M. 135
Reese, J.M. 132
Reiche, J.G. 135
Rensberger, D.K. 120n42, 144
Rigaux, B. 106n11, 118nn16,19, 126n52, 132, 144
Robbins, V.K. 109n40, 139-40
Roberts, W.R. 117n1, 140
Robinson, D.W.B. 135
Rockinger, L. 111n76, 139
Roetzel, C.J. 140
Rongy, H. 135
Roon, A. van 89, 125n43, 144
Rudolph, K. 144

Ruether, R.R. 140

Schade, H.-H. 122n13, 144
Schenke, H.-M. 145
Schille, G. 123n29, 125n45, 126n50, 145
Schlier, H. 124n33, 145
Schmidt, J.E.C. 15, 84, 105n2, 135
Schmidt, P. 122n17, 132
Schmithals, W. 135
Schnackenburg, R. 125nn39,46,47, 126nn50,56,58, 145
Schoedel, W.R. 127n7, 145
Schubert, P. 117n6, 145
Schweizer, E. 106n10, 122n21, 123n29, 126nn54,55, 135, 145
Scott, R.L. 136
Sider, R.D. 140
Siegert, F. 23, 108n38, 140
Smyth, H.W. 118n16, 145
Solmsen, F. 112nn90,92, 140
Spencer, A.B. 140
Spenger, L. 113n92, 140
Speyer, W. 127n9, 145
Spicq, C. 122n20, 127n7, 145
Staab, K. 132
Stählin, W. 135
Staerk, W. 124n31, 145
Stead, G.C. 140
Stephenson, A.M.G. 135
Stowers, S.K. 25-26, 108n36, 110n56, 111nn57,58, 119n29, 140

Taylor, G. 121n5, 141
Thompson, E. 136
Thraede, K. 109n43, 120n40, 140
Towner, P.H. 123n25, 145
Trilling, W. 16, 60, 105n2, 106n12, 126n53, 132, 136

Vacalopoulos, A.E. 145
Vielhauer, P. 122n21, 145
Vigna, G.S. 140
Volkmann, R. 112n89, 114n142, 140

Weische, A. 116n201, 140
Weiss, J. 20-21, 107nn13-19, 121n5, 140, 144
Welles, C.B. 116n204, 144
West, J.C. 121n5, 136

White, J.L. 24-25, 30, 110nn49-55, 65, 112n82, 140
Wilder, A.N. 140
Wilke, C.G. 20, 107nn9-12, 140
Wilken, R.L. 128n22
Wohlenberg, G. 132
Wooten, C.W. 116n201, 140

Wrede, W. 16, 80, 84-85, 102-103, 106nn5-9, 122n18, 128n19, 136
Wrzol, J. 136
Wuellner, W. 22-23, 108n33, 109n40, 141

Zimmer, F. 136

JOURNAL FOR THE STUDY OF THE NEW TESTAMENT
Supplement Series

1 THE BARREN TEMPLE AND THE WITHERED TREE
William R. Telford

2 STUDIA BIBLICA 1978
II. Papers on the Gospels
E.A. Livingstone (ed.)

3 STUDIA BIBLICA 1978
III. Papers on Paul and Other New Testament Authors
E.A. Livingstone (ed.)

4 FOLLOWING JESUS
Discipleship in Mark's Gospel
Ernest Best

5 THE PEOPLE OF GOD
Markus Barth

6 PERSECUTION AND MARTYRDOM IN THE
THEOLOGY OF PAUL
John S. Pobee

7 SYNOPTIC STUDIES
The Ampleforth Conferences 1982 and 1983
C.M. Tuckett (ed.)

8 JESUS ON THE MOUNTAIN
A Study in Matthean Theology
Terence L. Donaldson

9 THE HYMNS OF LUKE'S INFANCY NARRATIVES
Their Origin, Meaning and Significance
Stephen Farris

10 CHRIST THE END OF THE LAW
Romans 10.4 in Pauline Perspective
Robert Badenas

11 THE LETTERS TO THE SEVEN CHURCHES OF ASIA
IN THEIR LOCAL SETTING
Colin J. Hemer

12 PROCLAMATION FROM PROPHECY AND PATTERN
Lucan Old Testament Christology
Darrell L. Bock

13 JESUS AND THE LAWS OF PURITY
Tradition History and Legal History in Mark 7
Roger P. Booth

14 THE PASSION ACCORDING TO LUKE
The Special Material of Luke 22
Marion L. Soards

15 HOSTILITY TO WEALTH IN THE SYNOPTIC GOSPELS
T.E. Schmidt

16 MATTHEW'S COMMUNITY
The Evidence of his Special Sayings Material
S.H. Brooks

17 THE PARADOX OF THE CROSS IN
THE THOUGHT OF ST PAUL
A.T. Hanson

18 HIDDEN WISDOM AND THE EASY YOKE
Wisdom, Torah and Discipleship in Matthew 11.25-30
C. Deutsch

19 JESUS AND GOD IN PAUL'S ESCHATOLOGY
L.J. Kreitzer

20 LUKE: A NEW PARADIGM
M.D. Goulder

21 THE DEPARTURE OF JESUS IN LUKE-ACTS
The Ascension Narratives in Context
M.C. Parsons

22 THE DEFEAT OF DEATH
Apocalyptic Eschatology in 1 Corinthians 15 and Romans 5
M.C. De Boer

23 SECOND TIMOTHY
A PERSONAL LETTER OF PAUL
M. Prior

24 APOCALYPTIC AND THE NEW TESTAMENT:
Essays in Honor of J. Louis Martyn
J. Marcus & M.L. Soards

25 THE UNDERSTANDING SCRIBE
Matthew and the Apocalyptic Ideal
D.E. Orton

26 WATCHWORDS:
Mark 13 in Markan Eschatology
T. Geddert

27 THE DISCIPLES ACCORDING TO MARK:
Markan Redaction in Current Debate
C.C. Black

28 THE NOBLE DEATH:
Greco-Roman Martyrology and Paul's Concept of Salvation
D. Seeley

29 ABRAHAM IN GALATIANS:
Epistolary and Rhetorical Contexts
G.W. Hansen

30 EARLY CHRISTIAN RHETORIC AND 2 THESSALONIANS
F.W. Hughes